# Foundations of Betrayal

## *How the Liberal Super-Rich Undermine America*

By Phil Kent

Zoe Publications, LLC
P.O. Box 5294
Johnson City, TN 37602-5294

**Publisher's Cataloging-in-Publication**
*(Provided by Quality Books, Inc.)*

Kent, Phil, 1951-
    Foundations of betrayal : how the liberal super rich
undermine America / by Phil Kent.
    p. cm.
    Includes bibliographical references and index.
    LCCN 2007924397
    ISBN-13: 9780971985117
    ISBN-10: 0971985111

    1. Liberalism--United States. 2. Wealth--Social
aspects--United States. 3. Nonprofit organizations--
United States.   I. Title.

    JC574.2.U6K46 2007             320.51'0973
                                   QBI07-600089

**FOUNDATIONS OF BETRAYAL**

Cover design by Lisa Bilz

Library of Congress Card No: 2007924397
ISBN 9780971985117
Printed in the United States of America

TO MY GRANDSON

*Charles Philip Kent*

# TABLE OF CONTENTS

*"The gargantuan power of leading left-wing foundations is put in proper perspective in 'Foundations of Betrayal,' especially the example of how the politically correct environmental agenda is advanced. Phil Kent underscores that ideology usually matters more than charitable intent."*

Tony Blankley, editorial page editor, *Washington Times*

# ACKNOWLEDGMENTS

This author owes a great debt to my family for steadfast encouragement, especially to my wife Bonnie, son Philip Jr. and daughter-in-law Bebe.

Special appreciation goes to a wonderful support team that included my wise and patient publishers Leslie and Edwin Burley, publicist Wendy Guarisco, events coordinator Patti Peach and Lisa Bilz who designed the book cover. Augusta, Ga., attorney Charles R. "Randy" Sheppard was extremely helpful with research and editing assistance. Atlanta, Ga., Judge Craig Schwall Sr. and Morrow, Ga., certified public accountant D.J. Fulton also dispensed invaluable advice.

David Horowitz and the online DiscovertheNetworks.org have performed yeoman service by gathering a vast amount of tax-exempt private foundation research and "connecting the dots" between the wealthy foundations and the many left-wing and anti-American groups they fund. Reading its information initially motivated me to write *Foundations of Betrayal*. The Washington, D.C.-based Capital Research Center is also a valuable repository from which information for this book was drawn, and encouragement from its president Terrence Scanlon is much appreciated. Activistcash.com and Undueinfluence.com are among other valuable sources of online information utilized. I especially want to acknowledge the help of several knowledgeable sources in the foundation world who unfortunately must remain anonymous in order to protect them from the intolerant leftists who dominate that world.


Phil Kent

# PREFACE

Follow the money.

That wise adage has been painstakingly applied by Phil Kent with regard to his latest literary labor, *Foundations of Betrayal*. He has followed the billions of dollars that annually flow from the super-rich, tax-exempt foundations for misguided or evil purposes. Involved in his wide-ranging research was the patient sifting through of countless federal 990 tax forms to discover precisely what the super-rich foundation boards and presidents are doing to alter our culture and country.

Readers may be surprised to find that some foundations like Ford and Rockefeller have been undermining the United States for decades. The author dissects the agendas of these foundations, as well as the newcomers, who seek to do our nation and people harm. Ford Foundation underwriting, for example, of the 2001 United Nations World Conference Against Racism simply threw gasoline on the fires of anti-American hatred. The level of "charitable" support Ford and others have been giving to Mideast extremist groups is also cause for great concern.

Both the author and I attended the Henry W. Grady School of Journalism at the same time during the 1970s. We spoke out on the vital issues of that day, and in our own way still speak out today. Phil became an editorial writer at age 23 for the Augusta, Ga., *Chronicle* and went on to have an illustrious career in journalism and, for a time, on Capitol Hill. We happened to work for different U.S. senators in the early 1980s. We were fully "educated" in Washington on how big money equals power— and how those levers are used effectively, and by who, to affect change. I especially saw, when working in the U.S. Education Department during the Reagan administration, how good policies can be subverted or sidetracked by hidden forces.

Phil Kent calls the awesome power of the foundations and their vast financial resources an "invisible government." It truly is.

This book documents how left-wing foundations work overtime to change Americans' attitudes regarding a wide range of policy issues. Who would have thought, just 15 years ago, that the amoral elites would dare attack the foundation of Western Christian civilization— traditional marriage between a man and woman? Phil notes that "the last taboo" is even under assault by the "if it feels good, do it" juggernaut. Along with same-sex marriage, "progressives" seek to legalize incest and Lord knows what else. Phil Kent documents that such permissiveness is not just fueled by politicians or the media. They naturally play a role, but the enemies of traditional America must have big money behind them to change our nation's course. *Foundations of Betrayal* reveals they are getting it— big time!

The super-rich elites viscerally hate the America fashioned by our founding fathers— "one nation under God"— although they are usually discreet about it. Check the foundation websites, as the author has, to see how many support multiculturalism, multilingualism and essentially open borders policies that eventually will force the U.S. to evolve into some sort of multicultural version of Brazil. Many Americans are seeing first-hand the disastrous impact of uncontrolled illegal immigration on our wallets, wages, national security and culture. Our country's laws, political institutions and once-common tongue are being subverted by this foundation-led crusade, cheered on by their media allies.

This book comes down hard on the National Council of Churches, and it is well that it pulls no punches. Phil further issues a timely Paul Revere-like warning about the National Association of Evangelicals. There are many fine people in its member churches. Yet the NAE sells out when, as he reports, they allow "the grantmakers in the temple." Liberal Christians are taking money from the secular left-wing foundations— even from billionaire atheists— and then bend their beliefs accordingly. Many "houses of worship" now essentially promote The Gospel of Al Gore or The Gospel of The Kyoto Emission Treaty.

Gullible "green church" congregations (and many other Americans) are brainwashed to believe Gore's movie that, among other questionable claims, depicts scary 20-foot flood waves hitting everywhere from San Francisco to Calcutta due to "global warming." Never mind that a United Nations Climate Panel expects only a foot of sea-level rise over this century. (Moreover, sea levels actually climbed that much over the past 150 years.)

Phil documents how many single-issue organizations fueled by foundation grants are immensely influential and harmful. That's why he devotes an entire chapter on the radical environmentalist movement funded by the foundations. Their ultimate agenda? Dictatorial big government, more taxes and less freedom for Americans.

I believe this book to be the most definitive work, from a constitutional conservative point of view, on U.S. foundations and the subversion of America and the West since 1980.

Phil Kent is a "happy warrior." He believes that if more voters become aware of the dangers they face from these super-rich wheeler-dealers, the tide can be turned in coming years. He writes a final chapter— taking the title from Lenin— "What is to be Done?" and offers hope with suggested reform measures that informed Democrats, Republicans and independents could and should embrace.

William Safire, in one of his last columns, wrote:

*We are taught that pride in independence is arrogant except in the case of the weak. Its opposite, interdependence, is now the passion of the elites: As 'travelers of the world together,' we are members of one world, transfixed by the notion that national aspirations and powers should defer to a loose, global government driven by the power of world opinion.*

The elites Safire writes about mock patriotism and covertly or openly despise the U.S. and its bountiful free enterprise system that is the envy of the world. They worship the United Nations and pledge to fight "racism" or "fascism." In *The Great Gatsby* Nick Carroway finally remarks to Gatsby that his rich, amoral friends "are a rotten crowd." What an apt description of the foundations exposed in this book.

*Foundations of Betrayal* comes out before the 2008 presidential election. The timing couldn't be better. As Americans think about electing a president and members of Congress, let's also consider exactly who the hidden forces of this "invisible government" are and what they are doing. And why.

You won't finish *Foundations of Betrayal* without concluding that the United States is in serious trouble.

Now let's do something about it.


The Rev. John Roddy
St. Hilda's Church
Atlanta, Ga.

# WEALTH CONTROLS CULTURE
## CHAPTER I

*"The issue today is the same as it has been throughout history, whether man shall be allowed to govern himself or be ruled by a small elite." – President Thomas Jefferson.*

There were only 18 American tax-exempt private foundations 100 years ago. They have proliferated like Southern kudzu to over 16,000 and amassed enormous power rivaling that of the federal government and countries like Great Britain, France and Russia. Yet, sad to say, the mainstream media refuses to tear away the veil hiding their mysterious operations and corporate funding sources. It wasn't until 2006, when billionaire investor Warren Buffett's announced plans to give the bulk of his fortune to five foundations in annual gifts of stock, when public attention began focusing on the influence of these private foundations.

It is their amazing clout that is cause for concern, and the anti-freedom and even anti-American agenda many pursue should make patriotic Americans angry.

What are American foundations' total assets? The Foundation Center, using 2005 figures, estimates a whopping $500 billion. Just the assets of the Pew Charitable Trusts ($4.1 billion in 2003) exceed that of the world's largest banking institution.

Some 1.5 million entities, not counting houses of religious worship, are classified by the Internal Revenue Service as tax exempt under sections 501(c)(3) and 501(c)(4) of the federal tax code that define charitable organizations. They are, unlike for-profit corporations, limited to very little direct lobbying of elected public officials or their staff. They are barred from participating in elective political campaigns. Many, though, have begun designating themselves as "public charities," giving them more lobbying clout while pursuing their ideological agendas.

The vast majority of private foundations were started by successful business entrepreneurs to perform philanthropic work in fields ranging from education to scientific research. Steel magnate Andrew Carnegie's *The Gospel of Wealth* is a very good description of the way a charity ought to work. Foundation-led initiatives during the 20th century produced outstanding, results-oriented studies and projects. Many helped America's poorer citizens to the betterment of overall society. It is therefore amazing and upsetting how much of this noble intent and good work gradually became sidetracked and hijacked over the span of 100 years.

The Rev. Frederick Gates, a longtime advisor to the Rockefeller Foundation quoted in Raymond Fosdick's *The Story of the Rockefeller Foundations,* reluctantly but incredibly admitted that huge sums of money were committed for the wrong purposes:

> *If I have any regret, it is that the charter of the Rockefeller Foundation did not confine its work strictly to national and international medicine, health and its appointments. Insofar as the disbursements of the Rockefeller incorporated philanthropies have been rigidly confined to those two fields (medicine and public health) they have been almost universally commended at home and abroad. Where they have*

*inadvertently transgressed these limits, they have been widely and in some particulars not unfairly condemned.*

Of course, Gates' use of the word "inadvertent" is laughable. As this book underlines, there is nothing "inadvertent" about the countless grantmaking "transgressions" in pursuit of the foundations' ideological agendas.

One can only hope the historic investment of Buffet's billions signals a break from the major foundations' 20th century shift to the political left, and serves as an example to other philanthropists who may not want to start a foundation but who want to invest in others that pursue non-ideological missions.

## Founders' intent circumvented

Private foundations are a means of controlling wealth. But consider how many billions of dollars of federal taxes annually are shifted to the middle class in order to support the machinations of thousands of foundations that, in the large majority of cases, are now dominated by big government collectivists, globalists and radical leftists.

Many of these institution's founders would be horrified if they could have foreseen what their heirs and successors would be doing.

Reflect on the words of Henry Ford II, the son of Edsel and the grandson of Henry Ford and the head of the Ford Motor Company after the Second World War. In his resignation letter to his family foundation's board of trustees in 1977, he expressed total disgust with its new orientation:

> *In effect the foundation is a creature of capitalism, a statement that, I'm sure, would be shocking to many professional staff people in the field of philanthropy. It is hard to discern recognition of this fact in anything the foundation does. It is even more difficult to find an understanding of this in many of the*

17

*institutions, particularly the universities, that are the chief beneficiaries of the foundation's grant programs.*

Ford lamented that the foundation bearing his family name was rejecting the very economic system whose abundance made its existence, as well as that of all other philanthropic foundations, possible. Even a decade before his resignation, a cursory review of Ford grants reveal they were directed ever more generously toward the anti-"establishment" campaign of the political left.

Researcher Gary Allen (*American Opinion*, 1969) cited a few typical grants during the turbulent late 1960s under the presidency of McGeorge Bundy, all designed to reshape American society:

- $475,000 to the black separatists of the Congress of Racial Equality;
- A $630,000 grant to the Castroite Mexican-American Youth Organization, which preached revolution and racial hatred;
- A $175,000 voter registration grant to help elect the radical Carl Stokes as mayor of Cleveland;
- $315,000 to the National Student Association, long controlled by leftists;
- $100,000 to the pacifist American Friends Service Committee;
- A $1 million grant to establish separatist-oriented African studies in American colleges;
- $1 million to the globalist Council on Foreign Relations;
- $630,000 to *La Raza* ("The Race") a Hispanic group pushing an open borders agenda.

The Pew Charitable Trusts were also hijacked by new officers and trustees. Consider that Howard Pew's intent in establishing his first trust in 1957 was to educate Americans on "the values of the free market" and "the paralyzing effects of government controls on lives and activities of people." Former Pew program director Kevin Quigley told *The Philadelphia Inquirer* in 1998, "The donors would not only be rolling over in their graves these days, they would be gyrating at

18

very high speeds." Other big foundations eventually taken prisoner by the left are cited in chapter four.

The Bill and Melinda Gates Foundation is the largest in the world with assets exceeding $29.1 billion in 2006. However, the Ford Foundation— with assets of over $10.6 billion in 2004— is the activist leader among thousands of wealthy foundations that fund hard-core leftist and anti-American organizations and projects.

How does this compare with foundations on the political right? The Capital Research Center says Ford's level of grant awarding alone is approximately 15 times the amount of the three largest politically conservative foundations combined.

## The goal: Change America

Norman Dodd, chief researcher and investigator for the congressional Reece Committee on foundations, once observed:

> *Wealth controls culture...(F)oundations have used their wealth to change American culture to one of collectivism. If a nation is going socialist, it is not merely because of labor unions or street agitators; but, amazing as it seems to those who have not studied it, because wealth— improperly used— has altered the culture of the nation and led it to the left.*

Dodd emphasized this point well over a decade before Henry Ford II's disgust became public. His words couldn't ring more true when one studies the scope and power of not only the "old timers" like the Ford, Rockefeller and Carnegie foundations but the "new kids on the block" ranging from the Pew Charitable Trusts that blatantly push an environmental and "climate change" agenda to the William and Flora Hewlett Foundation, one of the top funders of U.S. abortion programs.

Rene Wormser, counsel for the Reece Committee, observed that foundations and the American companies funding them "constitute a fourth branch of government." He noted:

> *They are the consultants... the planners and the designers of governmental theory and practice. They are free from the checks and balances to which the three other branches of government ... are subject.*

Truly, the total impact of wealthy foundations on American education, the law, sex and culture, foreign policy, welfare programs, environmental policy— you name it— is incalculable.

Let's focus briefly on the subversion of traditional education, high on the agenda of the Carnegie and Rockefeller foundations for over 80 years. The Carnegie Corporation once spent $340,000 to develop and disseminate what the Reece Committee described as a socialist charter for education. This early 1930s project, prepared by the Commission on Social Studies of the American Historical Association, incredibly concluded:

> *Cumulative evidence supports the conclusion that, in the United States and in other countries, the age of individualism and laissez faire in economy and government is closing and that a new age of collectivism is emerging.*

Harold Laski, a well-known British socialist, praised the Carnegie-funded charter: "At bottom, and stripped of its carefully neutral phrases, the report is an educational program for a socialist America."

Congressional investigators found Carnegie continually made grants to pro-Communists typified by Columbia University Economics Professor Robert Brady. The foundation financed his studies and a book *Business as a System of Power*. The latest book cover displays a Communistic clenched fist holding a dollar sign, and its theme is summed up in the foreward:

*...capitalistic economic power constitutes a direct, continuous and fundamental threat to the whole structure of democratic authority everywhere and always.*

## The real 'Department of Education'

From their genesis, the Carnegie and Rockefeller foundations worked shoulder-to-shoulder in terms of both philosophy and staff. During the first third of the 20th century, according to author Ernest Hollis in *Philanthropic Foundations and Higher Education,* these two entities stimulated approximately two-thirds of the total endowment funding of all institutions of higher learning in America. Respected free market economist Ludwig von Mises once reflected on this problem in an open letter to a congressional committee:

*It is a fact that the intolerant practices of many university departments of the social sciences are lavishly financed by some rich foundations. These foundations are uncritically committed to the epistemological ideas and the political bias prevalent in the university faculties.*

The Carnegie and Rockefeller foundations functioned as a U.S. Department of Education decades before the Cabinet-level agency was ever formed. They religiously funded and produced textbooks promoting socialist John Dewey's permissive brand of education, prompting Reece counsel Wormser to conclude: "It's difficult to believe that....the National Education Association could have supported these textbooks." One notorious example was a Rockefeller grant of $50,000 to produce a public school textbook *Building America*. It was so controversial that the California legislature refused to appropriate funding for it and further issued a report stating that the text was designed to downgrade America and contained "purposely distorted references favoring communism."

U.S. Rep. Eugene Cox, D-Ga., particularly attacked the Rockefeller Foundation "whose funds have been used to finance individuals and organizations whose business it has been to get communism into the private and public schools of the country, to talk down America and play up Russia…"

Yale historian David Nelson Rowe, in testimony before the Reece committee, perhaps best summed up how the foundations had already turned American education leftward by the 1950s:

> *I think that the development of the social sciences in this country in the last 40 to 50 years has been heavily influenced, in my opinion, by ideas imported from abroad, which have been connected with, if not originated in, socialistic mentality… I think it must be kept in mind that the theory of social engineering is closely related to the notion of the elite which we find dominant in Marxism, the notion that a few people are those who have the expertness and that these people can engineer the people as a whole into a better way of living, whether they like it or want it or not…*

Almost 20 years later Dodd, in the November 1969 *American Opinion* article authored by Allen, told the author:

> *The principles upon which this country was founded are now held in scorn as the result of the changes fostered by the foundations' control of education. The foundations have been able to take the philosophy upon which American civilization was based and turn it into its opposite. The foundations are fostering under the guise of public spirited largesse, a theory and philosophy totally divorced from that of the Founding Fathers.*

## Big money no enemy of the left

A movement cannot succeed unless it has big money behind it. America's radical left is no exception. Historian Oswald Spengler foresaw what many American liberals cannot or don't want to see: A huge segment of the political left has come to be manipulated if not controlled by its supposed enemy— the super-rich.

Author Hilaire Belloc in *The Servile State* predicted that monopoly capitalism and socialism would basically, down the road, join hands to establish a new "servile civilization." Isn't that essentially the point Nelson and David Rockefeller made countless times whether talking with capitalists or Communists?

Why would some wealthy Americans want big government socialism or even a one-world government? Dr. Gabriel Kolko, considered a leading historian of America's "New Left," examined the big-government phenomenon in a 1963 book *The Triumph of Conservatism*— although he erroneously uses the term "conservatism" to simply mean big business. The professor's thesis (also held by some conservative economists) is that free enterprise and competition were vibrant in the early 20$^{th}$ century, so some big corporations reacted to the free market by working to forge "a government-business coalition" to protect their own "inefficiencies." In *The Triumph,* Kolko wrote:

> *... the significant reason for many businessmen welcoming and working to increase federal intervention into their affairs has been virtually ignored by historians and economists. ... Despite the large number of mergers, and the growth in the absolute size of many corporations, the dominant tendency in the American economy at the beginning of this (20$^{th}$) century was toward growing competition. Competition was unacceptable to many key business and financial interests.*

The best way for these super-rich to eliminate the competition was to make sure the tax laws helped them and hurt the competition, while creating and nurturing protective incubators for themselves— the tax-exempt foundation.

# Incomplete foundation probes

Congress first tried to seriously investigate and rein in the growing power of foundations during President Dwight Eisenhower's administration. Both efforts were noble but far too incomplete.

A probe was initiated in 1952 by none other than the aforementioned Congressman Cox. Warren Weaver wrote in *U.S. Philanthropic Foundations* that the Cox panel wanted to determine which "foundations and organizations are using their resources for purposes other than the purposes for which they were established, and especially to determine which such foundations and organizations are using their resources for un-American and subversive activities or for purposes not in the interest and tradition of the United States."

Cox's liberal colleagues delayed the appropriation of funds for the committee and then, when they couldn't kill it outright, managed to impose a six-month deadline to complete a complex investigation that naturally would have required several years. When Congressman Cox died during the probe, the panel lost steam and its final report was rushed and incomplete.

Taking up the investigatory banner was U.S. Rep. B. Carroll Reece, R-Tenn., one of conservative U.S. Sen. Robert Taft's 1952 campaign managers and a member of the Cox Committee. The mandate for the Reece Committee was the same as for its predecessor. Predictably, the mainstream media became hysterical and Eisenhower (who beat Taft for the 1952 GOP presidential nomination and went on to win the general election) was none too pleased. *The Washington Post* editorially said the 1953-54 Reece effort was "stupidly wasteful of public funds" and liberals in both the Republican and Democratic cloakrooms went to work to kill the probe. Reece Committee counsel Wormser particularly noted in a 1969 *Human Events* article the sabotage tactics of U.S. Rep. Wayne Hayes, D-Ohio:

> *Mr. Hayes showed himself exceptionally adept at disruption. He resorted to constant interruption 246 times, for example, in one session of 185 minutes. He refused to obey the rules of the committee. He insulted*

*... witnesses, counsel to the committee and committee members themselves. His intransigence finally caused a termination of the hearings.*

Furthermore, according to Wormser, "Hayes told us one day that 'the White House' had been in touch with him and asked him if he would cooperate to kill the committee." The Ohio congressman was particularly incensed that investigators wanted to probe foundation funding to the controversial Dr. Alfred Kinsey at Indiana University for allegedly flawed and distorted "scientific research" on human sexuality. Hayes even wanted the investigators' Kinsey file locked in his safe so it would never become public.

In the end, the Reece Committee could conduct only limited investigations of the Rockefeller, Ford and Carnegie foundations. Its funding was trimmed and then terminated by the end of 1954. Wormser lamented that powerful bipartisan forces ensured that the ever-growing influence of wealthy foundations remained mysterious. In its final report, the panel observed:

*It would be interesting to aggregate the total funds poured by the foundations into the dissemination of leftist propaganda and compare it with the trickle which flowed into the exposition of the fallacies and frailties of collectivism.*

It wasn't until the late 1960s when meaningful oversight hearings were again held by U.S. Rep. Wright Patman, D-Tex.— the chairman of the House Banking and Currency Committee. He pried information out of reluctant non-profits and exposed to public view how they could buy, sell or hold real estate and securities— something not well understood at the time. The Texas populist charged in colorful oratory how big foundations were acting in concert, wheeling and dealing in ways which used to be called "rigging the stock market." Little congressional reform occurred, however, as a result of his efforts.

# Foundations given more power

With Congress showing little interest in the control of foundations, and as the 21st century began, they received more power. Amazingly, it came from the IRS. Consider what has happened with the Pew Charitable Trusts and others.

A 2004 *Wall Street Journal* editorial analyzed how the Pennsylvania-based Pew Trusts changed their legal status from private foundation to public charity:

> *Here's the catch: Pew argued that its seven trusts should be counted separately to fulfill the charity requirement demonstrating broad public support. Incredibly, both the IRS and the Pennsylvania attorney general agreed— even though these seven trusts are centrally administered and share the same executive management... Pew's new status frees it up to spend money directly, to raise even more money, and to devote up to 5 percent of its annual $200 million budget to lobbying. That's a lot of (Washington) K Street lunches.*

The May 2004 issue of *Foundation Watch* expands on this point:

> *Public charities usually follow the so-called '20-and-5' lobbying rule: spend no more than 20 percent of the organization's annual revenue for direct lobbying (influencing legislators) and spend no more than 5 percent for grassroots lobbying (where the group urges others to influence legislators). Groups are subject to an excise tax if they spend more than permitted, and can lose their exempt status if they exceed the permitted amounts by more than 50 percent over a four-year period.*

> *So, following the IRS '20 and 5' rule, the 5 percent is only the grassroots portion of the allowance*

*(Pew gets others to influence legislators); Pew can now spend 20 percent for its own direct lobbying (Pew influences legislators). $40 million might even buy the K Street restaurant.*

*The Wall Street Journal* quoted the Foundation Management Institute's Neal B. Freeman: "It's the perfect vicious circle. With this tax change, trusts that were set up with money from the Sun Oil Company will now be used to lobby for a Kyoto Treaty whose primary victims will be America's energy companies." (In 1997 the U.S. Senate unanimously opposed by a 95-to-0 vote the emissions-cap treaty. President George W. Bush later stated, "I oppose the Kyoto Protocol because it exempts 80 percent of the world, including major population centers, such as China and India, from compliance, and would cause serious harm to the U.S. economy.")

## Dishonest 'philanthropy'

The "20 and 5" rule appears to be often violated. Consider just one example involving the Washington-based Environmental Working Group, heavily funded by the Pew Charitable Trusts, Ford Foundation, Turner Foundation and others. This greenie group is an example of the dishonesty currently running amok in the philanthropy world.

EWG produced the *Shoppers Guide to Pesticides in Produce* in 1996. The Environmental Protection Agency— and, remember, this was when the Clinton administration controlled the agency— condemned the work as "junk science" and EWG official Richard Wiles later conceded to investigative reporter Matt Labash that his foundation did not have a single scientist or doctor on its staff.

In 2002 the Center for the Defense of Free Enterprise filed a petition with the IRS to remove the EWG's tax-exempt status. The plaintiff presented a compelling case that EWG's lobbying vastly exceeded the "20 and 5" rule, including a $1.62 million grant from the Joyce Foundation for "work on the 2002 farm bill." Unfortunately, liberals in the IRS bureaucracy derailed the claim and the foundation continued its irresponsible attacks on everything from the pesticide industry (despite the minimal health risks from pesticides) to lumber companies (over the use of arsenic as a wood preservative).

The boards and presidents of many foundations are more Machiavellian than humanitarian as they pursue their own governmental agenda. They can't openly brag that they are the elite captains and kings and that everybody else on the planet are serfs. So left-wing foundations just crank up slick public relations campaigns, touting their politics-cloaked-in-good-works on behalf of the masses as the remedy for everything from environmental disaster to nuclear annihilation. A liberal president of the Council on Foundations, James Joseph, once advised using deception to his association of over 2,000 grantmakers:

> We must find ways to translate what we know
> into the policy options our public officials are debating,
> and we must do so without appearing to be partisan or
> political.

Of course, at the same time, remember that these super-rich are not divesting their wealth— they are protecting it from taxation and expanding their assets.

The next chapter will more fully explore how much of this is at the expense of our free enterprise system, traditional values and national sovereignty.

# THE INVISIBLE GOVERNMENT'S AGENDA
## CHAPTER II

*"The main obstacle to a stable and just world is the United States." – Billionaire George Soros.*

Former U.S. Sen. Bill Bradley, D-N.J., in a May 15, 2002 *New York Times* op-ed piece, wrote that foundations should be judged by their achievements, not by their endowments. "Their current strategy is especially harmful today," he co-wrote with Paul Jansen, "when some 13 million children live in poverty, nearly 41 million people have no health insurance and many urban schools are failing. The decision by non-profit groups to increase their endowments in the face of these needs suggests that, for some, the endowment has become an end in itself."

Bradley and Jansen worry about the direction major foundations are going while ignoring average Americans, especially the nation's poorer citizens:

> *The burgeoning federal deficit, coupled with new spending for defense and homeland security, will soon put health care, education and other social programs in a serious squeeze. Yet this crunch can be eased if the richest U.S. nonprofits groups distributed more of their money now instead of saving for the*

*future. They could provide the United States with some $20 billion more a year to spend on urgent social needs.*

The authors make an excellent point.

Foundations are required to distribute only 5 percent of their assets every year. Their governing boards and presidents, which could be donating billions of dollars more to address America's social and medical needs, instead doggedly pursue their own ideological objectives in education, science, domestic policy and foreign affairs in ways that harm the United States. They are hoarding and using vast resources to implement their own "invisible government" agenda. "Other urgent needs," to cite the words of Bradley and Jansen say, are lower priorities.

One example of a domestic need being ignored involves the Open Society Institute founded by George Soros. *Philanthropy Notes,* published by the Capital Research Center, discovered OSI never announced any post-Hurricane Katrina donations or related humanitarian programs until after Soros bought an expensive full-page anti-Bush administration advertisement in the Sept. 7, 2005 *Wall Street Journal.* The ad text concluded: "The devastation wrought by Katrina will inevitably lead to profound heart-searching. I hope it will start with a reconsideration of the 'war on terror.'" When asked about it, *Philanthropy Notes* says a spokeswoman initially responded that OSI "is not a relief organization" but later added, after more prodding, that some OSI response would occur down the road.

Such dissembling is a reminder of author Joel Fleishman's main criticism of the philanthropic world: It is basically arrogant, secretive and insular. The former president of the Atlantic Philanthropic Service Co. says big foundations latch onto trendy initiatives without ever evaluating the impact. There is all too often a herd mentality, with a liberal foundation funding a project already funded or identified by others— or there could be partnering on a project. There is no accountability, Fleishman laments, and thus they waste of untold millions of dollars annually. It harkens back to what Andrew Carnegie said, "Of every thousand dollars spent in so-called charity today, it is possible that $950 is unwisely spent; so spent, indeed as to produce the very evils which it proposes to mitigate or cure." And that was in 1889!

The Bill and Melinda Gates Foundation could be a prominent exception to this lack of responsibility, considering Bill Gates' fervent belief that he might have a real chance to find cures for the 20 leading fatal diseases. However, as Hudson Institute economist Irwin Stelzer points out in a July 17, 2006 *Weekly Standard* piece, very little of the Gates' giving in the health field will remain in the country that made his success possible. "As laudable as giving away such large sums might be, most of the money is destined for places far from our shores, and hardly constitutes 'giving back' to the system that made the wealth creation possible."

## For decades, an 'invisible hand'

If the super-rich foundations aren't primarily tackling our own nation's health care, poverty and educational needs, what are they focused on? The next two chapters detail what top left-wing foundations are doing *to,* rather than *for*, our country.

But first some history.

The big foundations and their financiers have been, since 1945, strong backers of internationalist groups— particularly the United Nations headquartered in New York City.

Public opinion polls in recent years show a majority of Americans have little or no faith in the United Nations. During the Cold War, the Communist-Third World majority in the U.N. General Assembly bloc-voted against American and Western interests. Since the fall of Soviet communism, some journalists and think tanks have documented how the large majority of U.N. members receive U.S. foreign aid yet usually vote against U.S. foreign policy interests. President George W. Bush, reflecting the national mood, once declared this country's sovereignty came first over the United Nations. No

American soldiers, he assured cheering 2004 Republican Party convention delegates, would serve under U.N. auspices.

An "invisible hand," however, pushes mightily in the opposite direction assisted by its media allies. And it is not the beneficent "hand" about which private enterpriser Adam Smith once wrote.

As far back as 1952, the U.S. House of Representatives Special Committee to Investigate Tax-Exempt Foundations concluded:

> *Substantial evidence indicates there is more than a mere close working together among some foundations operating in the international field. There is here, as in the general realm of the social sciences, a close interlock. The Carnegie Corporation, the Carnegie Endowment for International Peace, the Rockefeller Foundation and recently the Ford Foundation, joined by some others, have commonly cross-financed, to the tune of many millions, furnished intermediate and agency organizations concerned with internationalists (sic), among them the Institute for Pacific Relations, the Foreign Policy Association, the Council on Foreign Relations, the Royal Institute of International Affairs and others… and that it happened by sheer coincidence stretches credulity.*

A year after the founding of the United Nations, the Rockefeller Foundation annual report flatly stated: "The challenge of the world is to make the world one world … that will serve the welfare of mankind everywhere." That the Rockefeller Foundation has been continually undermining American sovereignty and our Constitution by pushing one-world government should come as no surprise. After all, their family's Standard Oil of New Jersey started as a huge oil operation that began operating in numerous countries and markets spanning the globe.

Banker David Rockefeller and brother Nelson— the late New York governor, vice president and longtime enemy of conservative Republicans— were often blunt over the years about putting the

United Nations above all. A typical example is contained in a July 26, 1968 Associated Press report: "New York Gov. Nelson Rockefeller says as president he would work toward creation of a 'new world order based on East-West cooperation.'"

## One world government a goal

The Rockefeller family and countless other limousine liberals are enamored with world government or what they often term their "new order" primarily because 1) their empires are worldwide and it is easier to control or manipulate a world body; and 2) their egos are colossal and they enjoy praise from politically-correct peers and the liberal media. Ted Turner of Atlanta immediately comes to mind in the latter category. In 1998 he pledged $1 billion to the world body. Since then targeted grant money has gone to the Turner-controlled UN Foundation which then turns around and gives it to the UN for approval and distribution.

Gary Allen, in a November 1969 *American Opinion* article, notes the U.S. House investigation in the 1950s found left-wing foundations acting as a "mid-wife at the birth" of various one-world organizations. Allen wrote:

> *The Foreign Policy Association, a 'prestigious' group which disseminates Communist propaganda, was referred to by the Reece Committee as 'virtually a creature of the Carnegie Endowment' for which it did 'research.' The research director of the Association for over 20 years was Vera Michaels Dean, a notorious Russian-born comrade.* The New York Times *of Oct. 14, 1969 quotes her as telling an audience of Americans they must 'whittle away their conception of national sovereignty' and pull themselves out of the 'ancient grooves of nationalism.'*

An influential organization hostile to American nationalism is the New York City-based Council on Foreign Relations. An objective look at this internationalist organization reveals that it has been consistently underwritten by leading foundations.

Established after World War I and the failure of the League of Nations, key CFR founders were John D. Rockefeller and bankers Paul Warburg, Jacob Schiff and J.P. Morgan. John J. McCloy, one-time chairman of both the Rockefeller's Chase Manhattan Bank and the board of trustees of the Ford Foundation, served as a CFR chairman. He was succeeded by none other than banker David Rockefeller. Among a few of the more famous CFR members have been Dean Rusk, Henry Kissinger and Alexander Haig, secretaries of state in the 1960s, '70s and '80s respectively. Former Presidents George H.W. Bush and Bill Clinton are also prominent among the approximately 4,500 members.

Critics accuse conservatives of being paranoid regarding accusations that the CFR works to undermine the Constitution and U.S. sovereignty. Yet there are many instances in recent decades, often involving CFR policy "trial balloons" raised in articles published by members in its journal *Foreign Affairs*, which justify such concerns.

Consider a recent CFR foray— a People's Republic of North America. How does one explain the vice chairman of its task force on North America, in a 2006 appearance before a U.S. Senate Foreign Relations Committee hearing, recommending a merger of the United States, Mexico and Canada into a North American Union? Dr. Robert Pastor coupled it with a proposal to expedite Latin American trucks crossing the erased borders via new toll superhighways running through Middle America. Pastor further advocated a "North American dispute resolution" super-court to issue rulings affecting all three countries. All of this and more is contained in an official 59-page CFR report.

This one mind-boggling plan alone, which clearly undermines our sovereignty, prompted Cable News Network commentator Lou Dobbs to remark that the political and academic elites typified by Pastor have "gone utterly mad."

# "An amoral new order"

The left pooh-poohs the idea that traditional marriage and the family are under attack. Yet just a cursory glance at American culture since the 1940s advent of the vile Alfred C. Kinsey and his institute— dedicated to trashing Judeo-Christian standards of morality— reveals that the heterosexual family structure has been badly battered. Check the gloomy statistics regarding the growth in abortion, out-of-wedlock births, divorce, sexually-transmitted disease and sexual dysfunction.

It was the Rockefeller Foundation— again, seeking to remold America— that launched Kinsey's "free love" research as well as the public relations machine which made him a media celebrity until his death in 1956.

A column by Col. Ronald Ray noting the 50th anniversary of publication of Kinsey's *Sexual Behavior in the Human Male*, appearing in the Jan. 19, 1998 *The New American*, placed in perspective how Kinsey and the foundation partnered for an amoral new order:

> *A recent Kinsey biography by James H. Jones, a Rockefeller grantee and former adviser to the Kinsey Institute, reveals that Kinsey himself was a sado-masochistic homosexual on a perverted mission. Trolling through homosexual bars and nightclubs, Kinsey gathered the subjects for his research, drawing disproportionately from those participating in sexual perversions and other criminal acts. Those acts were then portrayed by Kinsey as both commonplace and natural. Kinsey's mission, Jones writes in* Alfred Kinsey: A Public/Private Life, *was to free America from Victorian 'repression.' But his wider goal was an amoral new order— possible only if human life is unhinged from the divine.*

Kinsey's flawed studies, which would alter many Americans' views on marriage and sexuality, were touted as "scientific authority" by his Rockefeller-financed publicists. The editor of *Harper's* magazine actually wrote a Feb. 2, 1946 letter directly to the Rockefeller Foundation complaining of being shunted aside by other journalists seeking to write about the Kinsey book— due to be released two years later. Rockefeller money began flowing to Kinsey "about 1941"— eventually to the tune of $1.7 million between the 1940s and 1954— through the National Research Council, according to Dr. Judith Reisman in *Kinsey: Crimes and Consequences*. "One grant was made direct to Dr. Kinsey," the book notes.

The permissive "if it feels good, do it" philosophy continued to be pushed in the 1970s, especially on campuses, by the Rockefeller, Ford and other leftist foundations— but with a new twist. Homosexual "rights" was a new cause to be funded and promoted with an eye toward the eventual goal: civil unions and same-sex marriage. The foundation-funded Sex Information and Education Council of the United States (SEICUS) took up the lobbying where Kinsey left off with a media-savvy permissive "sex education" crusade.

And, of course, big foundations were on hand in a big way, beginning in the 1960s, to fund abortion-related projects and organizations and later gay advocacy groups (covered more extensively in the seventh chapter).

## The Council on Foundations

Assisting these liberal philanthropists with overall strategy, and the targeting of their wealth, is the Council on Foundations whose members' aggregate endowed assets exceed $74 billion. Its staff is ready, willing and able to address questions on everything from management tips to investments. Once an apolitical trade association, it fell into line with the course charted by the Ford and Rockefeller foundations. Its thrust has been ever more noticeable in recent decades: Less emphasis on giving to traditional charities and more on grantmaking with a political and ideological purpose. (As an aside, there are some conservative and Christian philanthropists that try working within this group.)

Marvin Olasky, in an illuminating essay titled "Philanthropic Correctness" published in the October 1992 *Heterodoxy,* wrote that "Ford and Rockefeller veteran" David Freeman became the Council's president in 1967 emphasizing "adult education" for foundation trustees and staffers. Translated, that meant foundations should work to secure liberal and so-called "progressive" trustees and staff, while easing out politically moderate or conservative trustees. Freeman told the Council's 1974 Annual Conference, "We need to look at all the laws on the books and change them." Along with that telling quote, Olasky provides another from that same conference. Radical environmentalist Barry Commoner bluntly told attendees: "We are all children of private enterprise. We're getting ready to bite the hand that feeds us."

A *Boston Globe* news story at the time provided an additional overall account: "At a convention of the heads of foundations set up by the Fords, the Rockefellers, the Pews, the Carnegies, the Kresges, the Mellons and other 'malefactors of wealth' for the purpose of giving away $2.5 billion to $3 billion of the profits of private enterprise every year, the message seems as much a departure as would be, say, a paean to capitalism by (Communist) Chairman Mao…"

Olasky further reflected:

> *Conference time was not the only time for political propagandizing. Council leaders also used* Foundation News, *the organization's bi-monthly message, to praise foundations that funded— in their words'— anti-imperialism, corporate responsibility, access to media and the rights of tenants, GIs, prisoners, workers, Third World communities and women.' This particular politically correct message even offered an apology and justification in advance for any inconvenience its radical objectives might cause: the need to 'be protective of the physical, social and mental well-being of mankind... will result in some limitations of our freedom as entrepreneurs, but the cost benefits to us as human beings will gainsay all of*

*these.* (When Rebecca Rimel was named executive director of the Pew Charitable Trusts, the *Foundation News* not only approvingly described her as an "activist" and "socially liberal" but celebrated her disregard of the intent of Pew's Christian founders. It pointedly reported that Pew "eliminated almost all their right-wing grantmaking.")

David R. Hunter, an Episcopal priest who previously worked for the National and World Council of Churches, was executive director of both the Stern and Ottinger Foundations in 1975 when he exhorted the Council's Annual Conference to "get into the fray more than they do" over issues like "the ascendancy of military institutions" in America and this nation's "undermining" of foreign governments, as well as the "equitable distribution of wealth and power." He symbolized the new and growing breed of leftist members who had gained dominance of a group that, 10 years before, basically eschewed politics at its conferences.

James Joseph, who succeeded Freeman as Council president, told a Stanford University audience in 1984 that decisions about investments of private pension funds should be made by "officials accountable to the public constituency." The goal should be "to build a secure and just economy" under a "new order." He performed as the perfect Machiavellian. An ordained United Church of Christ minister, Joseph advised his flock to be discreet in their march to the left. Ironically, Olasky quotes Joseph indiscreetly telling Council members: "We must find ways to translate what we know into the policy options our public officials are debating, and we must do so without appearing to be either partisan or political." (He may have had his eye on the IRS, but more probably that Congress might actually perform vigorous oversight of tax-exempt foundations.)

In 2004 Council leaders were continuing their cheerleading for the left. Before the November general election none other than Maxwell King, president of the Heinz Endowments, led an attack on critics of Teresa Heinz Kerry's extremist grantmaking. Two years later, he would be elected Council chairman.

# The rise of Greenpeace

As the Council on Foundations was moving leftward during the late 1960s and early '70s, then-Federal Bureau of Investigation Director J. Edgar Hoover was complaining that some of its members were providing "substantial financial contributions to New Left groups." They were, as environmentalist Commoner crowed, using their vast resources to chip away at the very country and economic system that had created their wealth. That era saw not only the Dawning of the Age of Aquarius, but the spawning of a wider left-wing, anti-free enterprise thrust by foundations and the groups they were founding and funding. One that sprang up in 1970 is today perhaps the most prominent force in the environmentalist/anti-nuclear wing of the "invisible government"— Greenpeace. It has a lengthy record of "civil disobedience."

"As its maiden act," according to the website DiscovertheNetworks.org, "the group of still-green activists set sail on a halibut trawler called the *Phyllis McCormack*. The crew— a motley collection of activists who shared a common affection for environmentalist rabble rousing— traveled from Vancouver, Canada, to Amchitka Island. As (Greenpeace activist) Bob Hunter explained in his chronicle of the journey, *The Greenpeace to Amchitka: An Environmental Odyssey*:

> *We had the biggest concentration of tree-huggers, radicalized students, garbage dump-stoppers, freeway fighters, pot smokers and growers, aging Trotskyites, condo killers, farmland savers, fish preservationists, animal rights activists, back-to-the-landers, vegetarians, nudists, Buddhists, and anti-pollution marchers and picketers in the country, per capita, in the world.*

The intent was to disrupt a U.S. nuclear test— completely in line with the group's pacifist and environmental bent. Greenpeace claimed the test would particularly hurt the local sea otter population.

Even though it failed in that crusade, it sailed on to other colorful ones. Rex Weyler, a draft dodger and Greenpeace biographer, admits the forecasts of imminent environmental disaster which the organization parroted were usually a myth. "There's no clear evidence that people will die," Weyler once said of the Greenpeace tendency to foment fear in the media by invoking junk science.

Greenpeace got its name, according to Hunter, when "somebody flashed two fingers as we were leaving a church basement and said 'Peace!'" When social worker and activist Bill Darnell added, "Let's make it a Green Peace," the group's founding members readily adopted the name. It maintains international headquarters in Amsterdam, The Netherlands, and has worldwide affiliates and offices including the Greenpeace USA headquarters in Washington, D.C.

The organization has become more irresponsible than ever, prompting co-founder Patrick Moore to quit. In his many writings Moore denounces Greenpeace for becoming "dominated by left-wingers and extremists who disregard science in the pursuit of environmental purity." And, he adds, it is "anti-human."

"Greenpeace activists threaten to rip the biotech rice out of the fields if farmers dare to plant it," Moore says. "They have done everything they can to discredit the scientists and the technology." He is referring to a nutritious strain of rice known as yellow or golden rice, invented in 2000 by means of gene splicing. It has proven to be a Godsend to Third World people afflicted by vitamin deficiencies and malnutrition. Yet Greenpeace blindly opposes new biotech technologies. The good news is that this insane stance has triggered a sharp membership drop, especially among the scientific and academic communities.

Greenpeace also evolved into outright anti-Americanism. Since the 2003 war that toppled Iraqi dictator Saddam Hussein, members have targeted the U.S. military supply chain to disrupt arms, food and equipment going to U.S. troops in Iraq. In the Netherlands and in Spain they attempted to block ships from delivering U.S. military supplies. Members once blockaded the home of Australian Prime

Minister John Howard, citing his support for Saddam's overthrow as their motive.

*Forbes* aptly describes this U.S. tax-exempt non-profit as "a skillfully managed business" well versed in "the tools of direct mail and image manipulation— and tactics that would bring instant condemnation if practiced by a for-profit corporation." That doesn't faze Greenpeace's supporters like the Rockefeller Brothers Fund, the John D. and Catherine T. MacArthur Foundation, the Bauman Family Foundation, the Blue Moon Fund, the Nathan Cummings Foundation, the Scherman Foundation and the Turner Foundation. Greenpeace has also drawn gifts from various Hollywood celebrities including the rock singers Sting, Tom Jones and Elton John, who have sponsored its "save the rainforest" campaigns.

All this money adds up to a huge operating budget. In 2000, Greenpeace collected $143 million in total revenues.

## Big money & climate change

"The invisible government" of the foundations, the groups they fund and the politicians that fawn over them are an incredible sight to behold. The grantmaking influence they exercise just in the important area of environmentalism and the related controversy over global warming is cause for great concern. U.S. Sen. James Inhofe, R-Ok., in an Oct. 3, 2006 Cable News Network report, said:

> *The fact remains that political campaign funding by environmental groups to promote climate and environmental alarmism dwarfs spending by the fossil fuel industry by a three-to-one ratio. Environmental special interests, through their 527s (political fund-raising entities), spent over $19 million compared to the $7 million that oil and gas spent through PACS (political action committees) in their 2004 election cycle.*

ABC-TV meteorologist James Spann, in a Jan. 18, 2007 web posting, makes a further salient point:

> *Billions of dollars of grant money is flowing into the pockets of those on the man-made global warming bandwagon. No man-made global warming, the money dries up. This is big money, make no mistake about it. Always follow the money trail and it tells a story. Even the lady at the 'Weather Channel' probably gets paid good money for a prime time show on climate change. No man-made global warming, no show, no money. Nothing wrong with making money at all, but when money becomes the motivation for a scientific conclusion, then we have a problem.*

> *I don't know of a single TV meteorologist who buys into the man-made global warming hype. I know there must be a few out there, but I can't find them.*

Author and Hollywood icon Michael Crichton, who weighed into the national debate on politicized science and, more specifically, climate change, concluded in *State of Fear*:

> *In the 35-odd years since the environmental movement came into existence, science has undergone a major revolution. This revolution has brought new understanding of nonlinear dynamics, complex systems, chaos theory, catastrophe theory. It has transformed the way we think about evolution and ecology. Yet these no-longer new ideas have hardly penetrated the thinking of environmental activists, which seems oddly fixed in the concepts and rhetoric of the 1970s.*

> *We desperately need a non-partisan, blinded funding mechanism to conduct research to determine appropriate policy. Scientists are only too aware whom they are working for. Those who fund research— whether a drug company, a government agency or an environmental organization— always have a*

*particular outcome in mind. Research funding is almost never open-ended or open-minded. Scientists know that continued funding depends on delivering the results the funders desire. As a result, environmental organization 'studies' are every bit as biased and suspect as industry 'studies'...*

## Undermining border security

Besides the groups that peddle fear and flawed science, a popular recipient of massive foundation money in recent years is the vocal open borders and "multicultural" lobby which backs amnesty for illegal aliens and massive foreign guest worker programs.

Along with the American Civil Liberties Union, two organizations often suing the federal, state and local governments which are attempting to control illegal immigration are the Mexican American Legal Defense and Education Fund (MALDEF) and *La Raza* (Spanish for "The Race"). The former is heavily funded by the Ford, Rockefeller and Tides foundations, as well as by the David and Lucille Packard Foundation, the Bank of America, General Motors and the Levi Strauss Foundation. Big *La Raza* donors include the Bill and Melinda Gates Foundation, the Ford and Rockefeller foundations, the Lynde and Harry Bradley Foundation, the J.P. Morgan Chase Foundation, the John and Catherine MacArthur Foundation, the Bank of America and the William Randolph Hearst Foundations.

The open borders lobby consists of numerous foundation-supported advocacy groups seeking to change the demographic composition and culture of the United States. One of the most militant of these groups is the National Immigration Forum, founded by civil rights attorney Rick Swartz and mightily assisted by Harriett Schaffer Rabb, a Ford Foundation trustee and co-director of the Immigration Law Clinic at Columbia School of Law. John J. Miller, writing in the October 1998 *Reason,* noted the cleverness of Swartz's coalition-building:

*In 1982 he strategically merged with the American Immigration and Citizenship Conference, a much older outfit that was made up primarily of white ethnic groups associated with Ellis Island (and legal immigration). This assured that the National Immigration Forum couldn't easily be tagged with the charge of representing only new minority groups looking for special favors.*

Of course, the Forum *does* lobby for special favors, including amnesty on behalf of the 15 to 20 million illegal aliens already here. It also opposes English as the official language of government, and objects to creation of a national security entry-exit registration system to monitor people from nations on the State Department's terrorist watch list. Miller notes this is because executive director Frank Sharry is farther to the left than Swartz, who he replaced in 1990. Sharry previously headed the Boston-based *Centro Presente*, which assisted Central American "sanctuary" movements that hid immigrants from the law and which supported the pro-Communist Sandinista dictatorship against the Reagan administration-backed *Contra* insurgency in Nicaragua.

The Forum— which received over $3.3 million in grants in 2004— enjoys primary funding from the Ford Foundation, the John D. and Catherine T. MacArthur Foundation, George Soros' Open Society Institute and even the Fannie Mae Foundation.

## Brainwashing and bullying

Foundation money is also bankrolling liberal and evangelical church groups in order to advance the overall agenda. For decades the National Council of Churches has been singing from the left-wing political hymnal and more recently the  National Association of Evangelicals is being influenced to brainwash congregations with environmental "creation care" propaganda, as documented in chapter seven.

What if corporations or elected politicians get in the way of the "invisible government's" agenda? They get attacked and smeared. The Rockefeller Family Fund and other foundations teamed up to fund an ongoing smear campaign against ExxonMobil and other companies who fight in the public arena in defense of traditional free enterprise. Agitators are sent to company shareholders meeting to disrupt proceedings and complain about "big profits." Companies like General Electric and British Petroleum have been attacked, greeted with radical demands that come at the expense of their products and jobs. Politicians who don't tow the line, of course, get targeted by the foundation's favorite academics and activist organizations, their media allies and the 527 political attack groups they fund. Well-known personalities like author Crichton, as well as scientists and journalists who question politically correct propaganda especially with regard to the environment, also find themselves quickly under fire. Several state climatologists, typified by Delaware's David Legates who equates climate warming with "climate alarmism," have been particularly vilified.

If these elite financiers cannot quickly get their way through bullying, elections or court rulings, they patiently wait until there are more pliable political officials and judges. All the while their "educational propaganda" and lobbying aimed toward the masses continues unabated.

Their "invisible government" is just as powerful as the federal government.

Wouldn't it be wonderful if the advice of former Senator Bradley were heeded, and these elites shifted resources to address and fund America's pressing economic, social, scientific and public health problems in more prudent and non-ideological ways? It won't happen unless the American people rise up and demand reform. After all, why would this elite class surrender their "invisible government" influence voluntarily?

The Ford and Rockefeller "old timers" are on a roll, as are relative newcomers like Soros, Teresa Heinz Kerry and a host of others devoted to pushing left-wing societal objectives. The next few chapters will shine the spotlight on them.

# FORD: LEADER OF THE PACK
## CHAPTER III

*"It's really like the legacy of Henry and Edsel Ford has been kidnapped..." – Michigan Attorney General Mike Cox.*

It is a tough call, considering the IRS estimates there are some 68,000 American foundations, but perhaps the most radical, ideologically driven of them all is the Ford Foundation headquartered in New York City.

Incorporated in Michigan in 1936 by conservative automaker Henry Ford and his son Edsel, a U.S. House Special Committee to Investigate Tax-Exempt Foundations (the Reece Committee) got right to the point about its origin:

> *The Ford Foundation affords a good example of the use of a foundation to solve the death tax problem and, at the same time, the problem of how to retain control of a great enterprise in the hands of the family. Ninety percent (88 percent, according to other sources) of the ownership of the Ford Motor Company was transferred to the Ford Foundation, created for the purpose. Had it not been, it is almost certain that the family would have lost control. The only practical alternative might have been to sell a large part of the*

*stock to the public or to bankers, or to sell the entire company.*

*The solution selected was to give away 90 (or 88) percent of the company to 'charity.' So that the greater part of the estates would be free of death taxation.*

*The 'charitable' transfers could have been made, of course, direct to universities, churches, hospitals and other institutions. But this would have put the donated stock of the Ford Company into the hands of strangers. For this reason, we assume, a foundation was created...*

It was a blueprint followed by earlier foundations and, in its growing years, it directed most of its grants to Michigan charities. The foundation gradually divested itself from the Ford Motor Company between 1955 and 1974 and is now unrelated to the company-run fund. The foundation headquarters moved from Michigan to New York City in 1953 and all of its revenue comes from investments in international securities. It doesn't accept money from any other source.

Edsel died in 1943 and after patriarch Henry died in 1947 a seminal turning point occurred. Inexplicably, the Ford family passed along virtually all oversight responsibility to the foundation's trustees. They appointed a study committee, headed by leftist lawyer H. Rowan Gaither Jr., which spent two years interviewing "experts" on how the foundation should address the problems of the planet.

The foundation's values and objectives changed as quickly as did its emergence as a national and international powerhouse.


## Leftward ho!

Columnist Raymond Moley (*Newsweek,* Jan. 9, 1956) noted that absolutely no one on Gaither's committee— including its five university professors— had any experience in foundation work. "It could hardly be a coincidence that the 'five areas' which they recommended for the foundation correspond, to a degree, to the academic departments which the professors had been teaching." Moley reported the committee's plan ruled out funding "medical research, public health and natural science on the vague grounds that 'progress toward democratic goals are today social rather than physical.'" That was the jargon of the day, meaning trendy liberal projects— both nationally and internationally— were going to be funded by these pseudo-intellectual elites seeking to remake the world.

Under the new Gaither committee dispensation to make "significant contributions to world peace," there was no specific mention of support for traditional Ford charities in Michigan— so grants there were sharply curtailed.

Support for the pacifist American Friends Service Committee, however, was one of Ford's major grant-making forays in 1951 and 1952, pushed especially by foundation officers Paul Hoffman and Robert Maynard Hutchins. During this time the AFSC was counseling conscientious military objectors and urging the U.S. to establish diplomatic relations with Communist China— while American soldiers were fighting in Korea against Communist Chinese armies.

In the field of "education" during 1952-53, trustees awarded $759,950 to something they called Intercultural Publications with a mission "to help maintain world peace." Journalist Alice Widener analyzed *Perspectives USA,* one of the publications of Intercultural Publications. She found its contents "largely culled from the small literary *avant-garde* magazines, which pride themselves on a lack of appreciation of contemporary American life as it is enjoyed by the vast majority of American citizens."

Another recipient during this heady early '50s spending spree was the Fund for Advancement of American Education. *The Biographical Dictionary of the Left* by Francis X. Gannon provides insight into the project:

> *Dr. Thomas H. Briggs, professor emeritus of*
> *Columbia University, served on the advisory committee*

*of this Fund but resigned when he realized he was wasting his time. Dr. Briggs found that the trustees had turned their responsibilities over to the Fund's administrative officers. Dr. Briggs testified about these men before the Reece committee: 'These administrative officers doubtless present to the board, as they do to the public, a program so general as to get approval and yet so indefinite as to permit activities which in the judgment of most competent critics are either wasteful or harmful to the educational program that has been approved by the public.'*

He further told congressional investigators that hundreds of thousands of dollars of left-slanted "educational" programs "to favored localities and individuals" were "not likely to have any wide or important influence."

Briggs was proven wrong on that last count, as the foundation in the decades to follow invested heavily in effectively undermining the underpinnings of traditional American education. Whole academic disciplines have been created with Ford money, most notably feminist studies and, more recently, homosexual and transgender programs.

## Ford funds pro-Communists

Ford Foundation support of a think tank called the Fund for the Republic was a scandal during the Cold War against communism. The foundation's extremism had become so pronounced that Ford executives Hutchins and Hoffman, in particular, had become almost daily targets of attack by popular nationwide radio broadcaster Fulton Lewis Jr. It was a time when many Americans were naturally worried about Communist infiltration of their government and the Soviet Union stealing atomic secrets. Nervous Ford trustees didn't like having a rare media spotlight focused on their activities, so in 1954 they sent Hutchins and Hoffman out the door. When departing, though, they left with a tidy $15 million farewell present.

This sum was used to establish the Fund for the Republic.

Hutchins lost no time in orchestrating a sustained attack on the federal government's loyalty-security program. He retained as the Fund's paid consultant the former head of the U.S. Communist Party, Earl Browder. At the same time, Columbia University professor Walter Gellhorn was given a fellowship by the Fund. This grant was a real eye-opener as to the direction that the Fund would take because Gellhorn was an open member of the National Lawyers Guild, which a Senate committee described as the "foremost legal bulwark of the Communist Party." Furthermore, Amos Landsman was named the Fund's press agent although he took the Fifth Amendment before a congressional committee when asked about his relationship with the Communist Party.

Gannon cites another radical project:

> One of the Fund's most ludicrous productions was a Bibliography on the Communist Problem in the United States, a 474-page compilation prepared under the direction of Clinton Rossiter. It was a travesty on scholarship that cost the Fund $67,000 before the volume was allowed to go out of print. But in its short life, Rossiter's sorry work found its way onto library shelves throughout the country as a 'reference' work. In another venture of book distribution, federal judges and college presidents received from the Fund free copies of left-wing books by Samuel Stouffer, Alan Barth and Telford Taylor.

In 1959 another dynamo was founded that would cut a wide and tumultuous swath: the Center for the Study of Democratic Institutions. Individually and collectively, Gannon noted, "those connected with the Fund and the Center represented…the highest echelons of opinion-molding and policy-making influences."

The Center served as the operating arm of the tax-free Fund for the Republic, merrily launching projects and issuing reports. One of its 1960s papers titled "Community of Fear" gravely warned of a U.S.

military takeover of the federal government if treaty accommodations were reached with the Soviets:

> *If things continue the way they are going, the possibility of a coup by the United States military is real. The general assumption that the American soldier is automatically responsible to his civilian masters might be rudely shaken were there a serious and clearly visible retreat on the world front by the American policy-makers.*

The Ford Foundation continued funding the Center and wasn't phased when, during the Vietnam war, its board chairman traveled to enemy territory: North Vietnam. In January 1967 the Associated Press reported Harry Ashmore paid fawning tribute to Communist North Vietnamese dictator Ho Chi Minh, saying:

> *I believe historically he will rank with Gandhi and it occurs to me there is nobody else in the world today in any country who seems to provide a similar blend of spiritual and political power.*

## The McGeorge Bundy era

McGeorge Bundy, once a Council on Foreign Relations analyst and later a top aide to President John F. Kennedy, assumed the Ford Foundation presidency in 1966 during the turbulent Vietnam and civil rights era. He strove to ensure the institution would be a left-wing horn of plenty.

The old-line liberal groups of the day were not neglected, including the National Association for the Advancement of Colored People (NAACP), the National Council of Churches (which was taking an anti-Vietnam war stand), the Pacifica Foundation which operated pro-Marxist TV stations and the Anti-Defamation League of B'nai B'rith. Degenerate black "poet" LeRoi Jones even received a Ford check. When called before a U.S. House committee overseeing foundations in 1969, Bundy repeatedly denied—during four hours of questioning— the foundation was involved in any way with politics. The Democrat-controlled Congress turned a blind eye.

By the way, all of this funding occurred *before* Henry Ford II resigned as a trustee over what he termed as the foundation's "drift to the political left."

The foundation was an early advocate of bigger governmental control over energy policy and William H. McIlhany, in his 1980 book *The Tax-Exempt Foundations*, focused on a major endeavor in this field:

> *In 1972 the foundation funded its Energy Policy Project with a budget of $4 million, out of which came during the next two years a series of publications, including a final report entitled* A Time to Choose, America's Energy Future. *While the work was done by a substantial professional staff, the 'final arbiter' of all issues was the project's director S. David Freeman, a bureaucrat who had not only made his ideology very clear in earlier reports but also had served as a primary staff architect for President (Jimmy) Carter's package of energy policy proposals. Carter thought so much of his work that he appointed Freeman commissioner of the Tennessee Valley Authority.*

McIlhany cites a devastating critique of *A Time to Choose* by UCLA Economics Professor Armen Alchian. The professor said the report "enters the Guinness book of records for most errors of economic analysis and fact in one book, is arrogant in assertions of waste and inefficiency, is paternalist in its conception of energy consumption management, is politically naïve and uses demagoguery." Consider the following excerpt from *A Time to Choose,* replete not just with socialistic governmental controls but the suggestion of "nationalization" (government takeover) of private companies:

> *Public desire for a stronger voice in the decision-making process affecting energy could be another reason for a more positive government role.*

*This role could range from more stringent implementation of existing regulations and programs to nationalization of certain activities...Federal chartering of the large integrated energy companies, which would open up corporate decision-making to considerable public scrutiny, has been proposed to the Senate, The federal charter would be a flexible device enabling the government to control various selected aspects of corporate activity. The appointment by the government of public interest members as corporate directors would be one means of public supervision. Corporations under federal charter also would be legally required to disclose the information on reserves and costs...*

*Another form of federal involvement would be creation of a federal 'yardstick' corporation. Following the example of the Tennessee Valley Authority in the electric industry, it has been suggested that a federal oil and gas corporation should be established that would explore, develop and produce oil and gas on federal lands. In theory this federal corporation would provide a benchmark for costs and prices, as well as a competitive spur to private enterprise to expand the search for oil and gas ... If the United States is determined to sustain rapid growth in energy, and yet fears the concentration of power in the energy industry implicit in such a decision, the establishment of a federal yardstick corporation is worth serious consideration ...*

*... (I)f historical growth is the nation's choice, and the energy industry repeatedly fails to satisfy the public's energy appetite within reasonable profit limits, nationalization is an option that may loom larger and seem more attractive...*

The report, among other recommendations, advised that "no (additional) nuclear plants beyond those presently operating or under construction" be built. (So much for clean, safe nuclear energy for electrical generation.)

Not all the criticism of these sweeping proposals came externally. A project advisory board member, Alcoa chairman John Harper, politely protested that the report "favors and encourages government intervention rather than the marketplace as the final arbiter of supply, demand, price, competition and profit." Another board member, Mobil Oil president William Tovoulareas took a hard shot aimed at project director Freeman:

> *Despite my consistent comments to the Project and the Foundation that the results were largely preordained by the Director's public statements and by the sources of the advice being received, efforts to obtain research in areas affecting the other side of these controversial issues were almost totally absent.*

Bundy, according to McIllhany, "loved the report." Fortunately, it soon gathered dust on shelves and almost all recommendations were ignored.

## Law schools & the ACLU

Another Bundy legacy is the radicalization of America's law school clinics, ostensibly to help "the poor." Heather MacDonald, in the Jan. 11, 2006 *Wall Street Journal,* wrote:

> *Law school clinics weren't always incubators of left-wing advocacy. But once the Ford Foundation started disbursing $12 million in 1968 to persuade law schools to make clinics part of their curriculum, the enterprise turned into a political battering ram. Clinics came to embody a radical new conception that emerged in the 1960s – the lawyer as social-change agent. ... (N)o one elected a Ford-funded 'poverty lawyer' to create a new entitlement scheme.*

In the area of civil rights and education, the foundation turned traditional liberalism on its head. The great liberal lion, the late Sen. Hubert Humphrey, D-Minn., declared that nothing in the 1964 Civil Rights Act, which he helped write, should be construed as giving preference to anyone. Bundy, instead of adhering to an "everyone is equal under the law" philosophy, ordered minority racial preferences to be requirements for grant acceptance. James W. Armsey, Ford's program officer in charge of minority higher education grants in the late 1960 and early '70s, complained about this in a June 16, 2003 letter to *The New York Times*:

> *After an exhaustive study of the needs and capabilities of potential grantees, I concluded that our grants should be based on class rather than race. My analysis and recommendations were not accepted. The conventional wisdom then was governed by an emphasis on civil rights and what became known as political correctness. We proceeded with grant patterns based on racial considerations.*

Perhaps the greatest "civil rights" endeavor of all, though, was that Bundy and successor Franklin A. Thomas— who served as president from 1979 until 1996— heavily financed the American Civil Liberties Union. The ACLU engages in a broad range of issues and, to be fair, its attorneys have achieved good results in some free speech and privacy areas. But its overall bent is clear. Labeled the "American Criminal Liberties Union" by former U.S. Attorney General Edwin Meese, local police have been hamstrung by ACLU-inspired court decisions related to arresting loiterers and aggressive street panhandlers. The organization believes obscenity is indefinable and therefore it merits First Amendment protection. Its lawyers live in constant fear that some locality somewhere will dare display the Ten Commandments or feature a Christian Christmas message. Chapters are also aggressively threatening and challenging many local, state and federal laws designed to restrict massive illegal immigration.

It also must be recalled, too, that one of the ACLU's first broadsides during in its early years was to attack Congress for investigating tax-exempt foundations!

"The ACLU has no better partner and friend than the Ford Foundation," gushed then-ACLU executive director Ira Glasser when presented with a $7 million grant in 1999. "It is fitting that the largest single gift... ever to the ACLU, should come from Ford."

## Public broadcasting born

Lawrence Jarvik's 1996 book *Behind the Screen* is an excellent history of how the Ford Foundation (with help from the Carnegie Foundation) in 1967 underwrote creation of our country's public television and radio operation, designed to compete with privately-owned news media. Ford's liberal TV consultant, Fred Friendly, believed there should be "public service" broadcasting (to be funded by both tax-exempt foundations and taxpayer money) in opposition to commercial television.

The foundation has long advocated that Congress impose special taxes to keep Public Broadcasting Service (PBS) programming afloat. That has not happened, but viewers will remember PBS's longtime star commentator was Bill Moyers, who regularly blamed corporate America and political conservatives for almost every ill or cover-up in America. (The Citizens for Independent Public Broadcasting speculates that PBS lost an estimated one million viewers during the 1995-2005 "Moyers golden age of liberalism.")

What to do to keep its child alive?

"Public TV and Radio to Receive Big Grants" trumpeted a May 10, 2005 *New York Times* headline over a story reporting that Ford was undertaking a $50 million, five-year initiative to support PBS, National Public Radio, a new PBS Foundation and "other media organizations" to spur public affairs programming. The *Times,* to put Ford's overall backing in perspective, reported that from 1951 to 1996 the foundation gave "more than $400 million to public media" (a large chunk for the programming selected and overseen by consultant Friendly).

Who is the executive director of the PBS Foundation which received $10 million in Ford cash? Veteran Democratic Party operative Cheri Carter. (So much for journalistic "objectivity.") Carter was once an aide to the late Commerce Department Secretary Ron Brown, served as chief of staff in the Clinton White House over the Office of Public Liaison and was chief operating officer for the 2000 Democratic National Convention.

## Suicide bombers funded

As the 21$^{st}$ century dawned, Ford's international political priorities could be categorized under the general theme of "combating racism" and specifically "understanding" and sympathizing with radical Islam. Population control is another huge grantmaking sector. In fact, Ford's website states that it surpasses any other foundation in the U.S. in international giving. Domestically, its main political goals could be described as "open borders" advocacy along with an enhanced focus on what it considers to be "protecting the environment." It selects a whopping 2,500 grantees every year.

President Susan Berresford, who took the helm in 1996, was determined to make her predecessors look moderate.

Between 2000 and 2002, Ford was the prime underwriter of the United Nations World Conference Against Racism held in Durban, South Africa. Held in September 2001, the U.S. only sent a low-level delegation after then-Secretary of State Colin Powell refused to attend. The confab was highlighted by verbal and physical harassment of white and Jewish attendees, with Ford official Bradford K. Smith crowing that the conference goals "have been at the core of the Ford Foundation's mission since its inception." Smith estimated that Ford would spend $10 million on what columnist George Will was to later label "a United Nations orgy of hate." R.W. Johnson, reporting for *The London Sunday Times,* further wrote that a parallel Ford-funded Durban conference of NGOs (U.N. non-governmental organizations) was also conducted in an atmosphere of anti-American and anti-white rhetoric.

Investigative journalist Edwin Black calculates that $35 million in Ford funds went to "Arab and Palestinian groups" between 2001 and 2003. Black also found several million dollars flowing to American and Israeli "peace" organizations.

Specifically, during 2001-2003, Ford gave $350,000 to the Al Mezan Center for Human Rights. DiscovertheNetworks.org notes that the Center's specialty is disrupting Israeli army anti-terrorism missions and lending material support, through association with the International Solidarity Movement, to Palestinian suicide bombers. Between 2001 and 2002, $135,000 was sent to the Health, Development, Information and Policy Institute, which advocates the boycotting of Israeli goods. Another $200,000 went in 2001 to the Haifa-based, America-hating Itiijah organization that played a prime role in the aforementioned Durban "racism" conclave.

From 2000-2002 Ford flouted U.S. foreign policy objectives by directing $700,000 to the Palestinian Non-Governmental Organization Network (PNGO), which consisted of some 90 localized operations in Gaza and the West Bank controlled by the corrupt and thuggish Fatah Party, an important component of the Palestine Liberation Organization headed by then-President Yasir Arafat. It should have come as no surprise to Berresford or Ford board members when President Bush felt compelled to sign an executive order barring U.S. tax-exempt foundations from providing further funding to this non-governmental network because of terrorist links.

Another non-profit recipient, the Palestinian Committee for the Protection of Human Rights (known as LAW), received $1.1 million from 1997-2001 according to journalist Black. He wrote that LAW "took leadership positions of the Durban conference steering committees, conducted workshops and even sponsored a pre-conference mission to the West Bank and Gaza Strip for South African delegates to convince them that Israel was an apartheid state."

LAW was also the target of a 2002 corruption probe after complaints from donors— including Ford itself, the Swedish branch of Save the Children and the governments of Canada and Luxembourg. Black was again breaking the story when the respected

Ernst & Young accounting firm was retained to audit the LAW books (underwritten mainly by Ford money). The result? Ernst & Young found nearly 40 percent of the $9.6 million that Ford donated over a five-year period was "either ineligible, unsupported, misappropriated or never spent on programs." Black reported another $2.3 million was "retained" by LAW with segments going for travel and "lavish hospitality." An Ernst & Young official at the time, *Foundation Watch* said, termed the whole LAW funding arrangement "ghoulish."

In 2002 the U.S. Agency for International Development began requiring U.S. charities dispensing grants to Palestinians to certify in writing that no money was going to "advocate or support terrorist activities." *Foundation Watch* in June 2004 reported, though, that "Ford seals all records of the grants it makes until ten years after the grant ends. That means that any evidence that Ford funds are being used for terror is locked in Ford file cabinets."

These revelations, which were finding their way into the mainstream media, embarrassed even longtime Ford sympathizers in Congress. The foundation was further threatened with a potential bipartisan congressional investigation. This finally forced Berresford to write a Nov. 17, 2003 letter to U.S. Rep. Jerrold Nadler, D.-N.Y. claiming "the Foundation has not and would never knowingly fund any group that advocates violence or denies the legitimacy of Israel's existence." (For a long time the letter was featured on the Ford website.) Berresford, while never fully apologizing for funding this extremism, further scurried (two years later) to reassure Congress over the funding of the Durban hatefest. "We now recognize that we did not have a complete picture of the activities, organizations and people involved," she wrote in that same letter.

Ironic, too, was that in October 2004 the ACLU— of all outfits — was also feeling the heat. It made headlines by rejecting $1.15 million from the Ford and Rockefeller foundations, saying it wanted to ensure that none of the money underwrote terrorism. The ACLU also returned $68,000 it previously accepted from Ford for the same reason.

# More Berresford extremism

Berresford once mused "whether we can do better" in somehow addressing Islamic extremists who seek to kill Americans, according to DiscovertheNetworks.org. That's no doubt why $300,000 went in 2002 to Fenton Communications, whose extensive work in the radical environmental arena is documented in the fifth chapter. This particular grant, however, went "to promote informed voices in response to the September 11th attacks, with an emphasis on the protection of civil liberties and prevention of discrimination." The firm directed by Fenton, who also headed the September 11th Families for a Peaceful Tomorrow, undertook with Ford Foundation money a massive media campaign basically blaming America for provoking radical Muslims.

Seemingly obsessed with U.S. "profiling" of Muslims in a war conducted by Muslims against the West, the foundation gave $150,000 to the Center for Constitutional Rights for "racial justice litigation, advocacy and educational outreach activities related to the detention and profiling of Arab-Americans and Muslims following the World Trade Center attack."

In 2002 the foundation funneled $100,000 to the National Immigration Project of the National Lawyers Guild "as core support for activities to ensure the human rights of non-citizens detained in the United States in the aftermath of the attacks of September 11, 2001." The Guild, originally that "bulwark" of the Communist Party, began specializing in defending Islamic Taliban soldiers held by the U.S. at Guantanamo Bay.

Look no further than to Ford, too, for providing the seed money to form and grow the Mexican American Legal Defense and Education Fund (MALDEF), a premier immigrant advocacy group. DiscovertheNetworks.org found that MALDEF received over $25 million since 1968. Nearly half of that giving occurred since 2000, when the group ratcheted up lobbying for "civil rights" and amnesty for millions of illegal aliens who snuck across U.S. borders. MALDEF also specializes in suing states and communities that pass laws mandating immigration control.

Ford's website highlights its support of other friendly foundations as well as a gaggle of political advocacy groups such as the National Immigration Forum, the Migration Policy Institute, the Immigrant Workers Citizenship Project, the Lesbian and Gay Immigration Rights Task Force, the University of Texas (for a Mexican border "philanthropy" project), Swarthmore College for "Islamic studies" and Emory University for "Islamic and black studies." Hundreds of similar recipients could be listed, but space doesn't permit it.

## Corporate America targeted

The foundation's long war against America's free enterprise system intensified under Berresford's presidency. Ford's heavy artillery is impressive, especially when you consider it shelled out $36.3 million from 1989 to 2005 to the Tides Foundation/Center for radical environmental projects, propaganda and lawsuits against corporate America. Consider, too, this partial list of hefty grants to these environmental advocacy groups cited in the fifth chapter:

- $4.7 million to the Rainforest Alliance (1997-2004)
- $3.9 million to Environmental Defense (1993-2001)
- $3.3 million to the Environmental Working Group (1989-1998)
- $2.7 million to the Natural Resources Defense Council (1989-1998)
- $2.2 million to Friends of the Earth (1993-2003)
- $1.8 million to Public Citizen (1997-2004)
- $1.6 million to the National Wildlife Federation (1993-2004)
- $1.5 million to the Union of Concerned Scientists (1999-2001)
- $875,000 to the Wilderness Society (1993-1999)

What does some of this money support? Consider one example from DiscovertheNetworks.org involving the Rainforest Alliance. RAN members in 2004 attacked the Weyerhaeuser logging company for cutting in old-growth forests. RAN activists even scaled one of the company's downtown Seattle construction platforms to hang a 2,400-foot protest banner. Five years earlier, in the same city, RAN members were prominent during violent rioting at the World Trade Organization meeting. Then-RAN executive director Kelly Quirke was blunt in explaining that demonstrators were warring against "capitalism." RAN founder and president Randy Hayes calls capitalism "an absurd system rapidly destroying nature"— and went off the deep edge by joining former U.S. Rep. Cynthia McKinney, D-Ga., in claiming the Bush administration deliberately allowed the Sept. 11 attacks on the U.S. to occur.

Another example is the Environmental Working Group, which received an individual $250,000 grant in 1993 for "a research and education program designed to inform policy makers and the public about the environmental consequences of pesticide policies." Consider the ramifications of such a program not just in this country, but in the underdeveloped Third World. Banning the use of the pesticide DDT condemns tens of millions of Asian, African and Latin American children to death. Such a result is particularly tragic, in view of the fact that scientific evidence does not prove that DDT is the carcinogen that radicals claim it to be.

## A new Ford direction?

Significantly, in September 2006, the foundation announced that Berresford would retire in January 2008 at age 65. "One of the challenges facing the board is whether they continue to follow their tradition or follow one of these new models," says Diana Aviv, chief executive of the Independent Sector which represents non-profits. The "new model" is a reference to the Bill and Melinda Gates Foundation, with its more results-oriented giving and tougher processes to determine grant eligibility.

When Ford's board announced Berresford's departure, Michigan Attorney General Mike Cox was into his first year of investigating the foundation— and garnering favorable publicity. He questioned whether or not some of the foundation's activities constituted political lobbying contrary to provisions of the Internal Revenue Code. He addressed foundation governance and potential conflicts of interest involving trustees. Cox further criticized what he termed insufficient support for the poor and working-class residents in the foundation's birthplace state of Michigan and its capital of Detroit.

"It's really like the legacy of Henry and Edsel Ford has been kidnapped," the attorney general told *The Detroit News,* "and we have an obligation to make sure they aren't plundering, that they aren't engaged in limitless self-dealing without parameters."

Daniel Howes, in his April 2, 2006 *Detroit News* column, wrote:

> *The foundation, which calls itself a 'public trust,' says its board delegates grant approval authority 'to the president and other staff and then reviews the actions.'*

> *Interesting question: The foundation's grant database says the foundation has awarded grants totaling $1.84 million to the Council on Foundations over the past three years. Berresford sits on the Council on Foundations' board.*

> *Foundation board chairwoman Kathyrn Fuller was CEO of the World Wildlife Fund for 16 years until she stepped down in January 2005. Between 2003 and 2005, the foundation awarded grants totaling $830,000 to the World Wildlife Fund...*

> *The Ford Foundation's ethics policy, revised in 2003, outlines specific rules for situations like these. Trustees are bound to acknowledge specific conflicts*

*and must recuse themselves from discussions about*
*potential grants. But do they?*

Cox's Michigan investigation, ongoing as this book goes to press, led *The Wall Street Journal* (Oct. 1, 2006) to speculate that Berresford's retirement might be "setting the stage for a period of soul-searching." In fact, if nothing else, the probe and the resulting local media attention have prompted Ford to sheepishly begin donating to some long-neglected Michigan charities.

Ford's financial clout is awesome. In 2005 assets were valued at over $11.5 billion, with a grant budget of over $622 million per year (or 5.7 percent of average assets). According to its website, it dispenses grants in the U.S. and 50 other countries and maintains offices in Asia, Africa, the Middle East, Latin America and Russia.

Maybe as Ford's record becomes better known— ranging from funding the proponents of junk science to violent Mideast extremists — a day of reckoning will finally arrive for the leader of the radical foundation pack.

# MORE TOP LEFT-WING FOUNDATIONS
## CHAPTER IV

*"It's hard to get rid of the money in a way that does more good than harm. One of the ways is to subsidize people who are trying to change the system and get rid of people like us." – Laura Rockefeller Chasin, a third-generation Rockefeller.*

There are thousands of left-wing foundations working to shift America's dialogue and direction away from our traditional culture and private enterprise system. With the Ford Foundation as the unofficial godfather, consider the following prominent players:

## Bullitt Foundation

The founder of the King Broadcasting Company, Dorothy S. Bullitt, established her Seattle-based foundation in 1952. Its mission is laudable: "Protect, restore and maintain the natural physical environment of the Pacific Northwest for present and future generations." While it has performed some admirable grantmaking in the area of conservation, Bullitt's good works are far outweighed by massive donations in recent years to radical groups and projects.

Bullitt died in 1989 and Denis Hayes has been president of the foundation since 1992. A co-founder of the Earth Day celebration, a university professor, an environmental lawyer and board member of the Nuclear Control Institute, Hayes is an unabashed opponent of capitalism. In his warped worldview, international communism— which murdered and starved untold millions in the 20th century— may not have been so bad compared to capitalism. And big government is the answer to what he labels capitalism's "flaw." "Under communism," Hayes writes, "prices were not allowed to reflect economic reality. Under capitalism prices don't reflect ecological reality. In the long run the capitalist flaw— if uncorrected— may prove to be more catastrophic." His solution is government, "the realm in which we decide what is dispensable and what is— literally— priceless." Government control is needed because "the richer the society, the more creatures it squeezes to the brink of extinction"— no doubt why Hayes donates to Democrat candidates friendly to more control over Americans' lives.

One of the foundation's program areas on its website is "Energy and Climate Change." It is committed to the "ultra-efficient use of energy sources" that are "safe, renewable and relatively benign in their environmental impacts." So far, so good. But the program further solicits money to encourage media attention to the importance of climate and other environmental impacts of outdated energy policies." In this context, Bullitt was a longtime underwriter of the now-closed Environmental Media Services, a creation of the public relations firm Fenton Communications. EMS was naturally far from objective in its "media pitches." (Fenton's firm pops up occasionally in the foundation world because of the fear-mongering publicity it generates.)

The online ActivistCash.com reveals Fenton's dirty secret: The "non-profit" EMS existed just to generate more cash flow. "It turns a profit for Fenton Communications by improving the bottom line of a wide variety of Fenton clients."

One of Fenton's clients, for example, was Ben and Jerry's Ice Cream. A March 17, 2004 FrontPageMag.com story explained that Fenton once spoon-fed its media allies the line that cows treated with hormones to produce extra milk could cause cancer or other maladies — never mind that the Food and Drug Administration labeled the hormone "entirely safe." Ben & Jerry's, you see, has ice cream made with hormone-free milk, so Fenton figured a good scare would drive consumers to the "alternative product" sold by his client. This is the type of flim-flam the Bullitt Foundation eggs on.

The foundation has also attacked private citizens and property owners in the logging, ranching and mining industries. The website Undueinfluence.com documents, for example, three Bullitt grants to the Tides Center that targeted Ferry County, Washington, for an orchestrated anti-business crusade. One grant was simply described to "counter anti-environmental rhetoric that promotes incivility."

Among major leftist grant recipients are the Tides Center ($1.4 million between 1993 and 2002), Greenpeace International ($21,500 during 2000 and 2002 alone) and just about every organization listed in the next chapter. Moreover, National Public Radio is also funded by this foundation, a circumstance that throws considerable light upon the manner in which it covers environmental controversies.

Bullitt's assets in 2004 totaled $98.8 million; that same year it awarded $4.3 million in grants.

## Carnegie Group

Steel magnate Andrew Carnegie compiled one of the biggest fortunes in American history and founded several entitles including the Carnegie Corporation, the Carnegie Foundation and the Carnegie Endowment for International Peace (CEIP). There's no question he was one of the great philanthropists of his age. Yet, since 1910, Carnegie enterprises worked with the Rockefellers in terms of philosophy and employing the same staff and consultants. As noted in the first chapter, socialist Carnegie programs and projects were at the center of subverting public education for much of the 20th century.

Biographer David Nasaw writes that big political donor Carnegie was obsessed with schemes and strategies for internationalism and "world peace." He was incessantly writing to and meeting with U.S. presidents who often privately grew weary of his attempts at international diplomacy which were frequently at odds with White House policy.

From 1910 until 1925 Elihu Root was the president of CEIP, and from 1925 to 1945 onetime Columbia University president and liberal Republican Nicholas Murray Butler was at the helm. Both were committed socialist one-worlders. The Reece Committee summarized CEIP's program:

> *An extremely powerful propaganda machine was created. It spent many millions of dollars in: The production of masses of material for distribution; the creation and support of large numbers of international policy clubs and other local organizations at colleges and elsewhere; the underwriting and dissemination of many books on various subjects…*

In 1934 the CEIP *Yearbook* bragged it "was becoming an unofficial instrument of international policy, taking up here and there the ends of and threads of international problems and questions." *The Biographical Dictionary of the Left* notes it was no idle boast: "Personnel from the CEIP and Council on Foreign Relations, which was subsidized by the CEIP, took consultative and administrative positions in the State Department during the 1930s and '40s." The man who succeeded Butler in 1947 at CEIP was none other than Alger Hiss, who served as interim general secretary of the United Nations during its formation and who was later exposed as a Soviet spy.

To be fair, Carnegie money funded exccllent educational pursuits in the early years. Joel Fleishman in *The Foundation: A Great American Secret* cites the recommendations of the Flexner report (funded by Carnegie) which led to a beneficial reinvention of U.S. medical education in the early 20th century. But, like all the foundations featured in this book, the Carnegie dark side eclipses such successes.

Carnegie money for years subsidized and controlled the American Council on Education along with various encyclopedias, including the prestigious *Encyclopedia of Social Sciences*. As the Reece Committee noted:

> *What is amazingly characteristic of the Encyclopedia is the extent to which articles on 'left' subjects have been assigned to leftists; in the case of subjects to the "right,' leftists again have been selected to describe and expound them.*

Carnegie entities duplicate Rockefeller funding in many sectors. Today, they especially subsidize educational television, student exchanges and open borders groups including the Mexican American Education and Legal Defense Fund and *La Raza*.

## Heinz Endowments

When it comes to hijacking a foundation, Teresa Heinz Kerry — the erratic wife of U.S. Sen. John Kerry, D-Mass.— is proof that life sometimes places someone at the right time in the right place. She dominates the Heinz Endowments in Pittsburgh, made up of the Vira I. Heinz Endowment and the Howard Heinz Endowment that share the same website, address and ideology. How did that happen? The Heinz family food fortune— over a billion dollars— simply fell into her grasp when her first husband John, also a U.S. senator representing Pennsylvania, died in a 1991 accident.

Kerry pushed grant-making to the left, particularly favoring radical environmental and "social justice" groups that supported her current husband's 2004 presidential bid. Over a million dollars have been given by Heinz entities in recent years to the League of Conservation Voters and, according to DiscovertheNetworks.org, "a number of (Heinz) executives sit on the League's 24-member board of directors." Represented on the LCV board are the Natural Resources Defense Council, the Wilderness Society, the Environmental Defense Fund (on whose board Mrs. Kerry sits) and the West Harlem Environmental Action.

Its federal 990 tax records indicate that in recent years the Vira I. Heinz Endowment has given grants to the Izaak Walton League of America, the Carnegie Foundation, the Environmental Defense Fund, the Brookings Institution, the Nature Conservancy, the Waterkeeper Alliance, the EcoLogic Development Fund and the Green Building Alliance.

Author Ben Johnson in *57 Varieties of Radical Causes* lists Mrs. Kerry's family foundation grant to the Massachusetts Immigrant and Refugee Advocacy Coalition. He notes that in 2002 MIRA instructed its members, "please do NOT aid people in applying with the INS (Immigration and Naturalization Service) unless you are familiar with their immigration history and are certain they would not be at risk of deportation by doing so." (Emphasis theirs) Johnson further found that after the Sept. 11 attacks it asked people to "refer local Arab, Muslim and affiliated groups to MIRA."

Mrs. Kerry has also given more than $8 million in recent years to both the Tides Foundation and Tides Center to further her open borders and environmental worldview.

Assets of the Vira I. Heinz Endowment totaled $466 million in 2004. Money awarded that year totaled $24.6 million.

## John D. and Catherine MacArthur Foundation

The MacArthur Foundation was formed by John D. MacArthur and his wife shortly before his death in 1978. John D. was one of the three richest men in the United States that year, primarily by having been the sole owner of the highly successful Bankers Life and Casualty Company.

MacArthur was a patriotic businessman who once mocked as "bearded jerks" and "obstructionists" the type of radical environmentalists his foundation now funds. Sad to say, he never defined the philosophy for his foundation. Witnesses say MacArthur actually exclaimed to his attorney upon its formation: "I figured out how to make the money. You fellows will have to figure out how to spend it."

That mistake inevitably led to an internal right-left internal slugfest between 1979 and 1981 over MacArthur spending, as recounted by DiscovertheNetworks.org:

> *Two of the original members of the foundation's board of trustees were the late conservative William Simon (who served as secretary of the Treasury during the Nixon-Ford administration), and the conservative radio broadcaster Paul Harvey. But when William Simon tried unsuccessfully to oust fellow board member Rod MacArthur (John's son, a leftist and a World War II draft dodger), Simon resigned, and the foundation's leftward course was essentially sealed. The foundation's current president, Jonathan Fanton, is the chairman of the Human Rights Watch.*

MacArthur assets totaled over $4.5 billion in 2004 and dozens of recent grant recipients are a long politically correct list ranging from homosexual rights groups to feminists and gun control advocates. It is a member of the aforementioned Peace and Security Funders Group and supports the anti-business Energy Foundation.

MacArthur originally bankrolled (with the Rockefeller Foundation) the Energy Foundation and it now has assets of $50 million; its seven constituent foundations list over $23 billion in combined money. This enterprise proclaims in its 2002 annual report that "reliance on fossil fuels endanger public health" and even "jeopardizes national security." What it doesn't want known is something *Foundation Watch* puts into perspective: "Regardless of one's opinion on global warming, one thing is certain: the technology simply doesn't exist to support a modern industrial economy based on non-fossil fuels." Electric reliability, to give just one example, would collapse in the U.S. if Hewlett and the Energy Foundation's polices were to be adopted.

No truer words were ever spoken than when high-ranking MacArthur official John Corbally said in 1987 that if John MacArthur were still alive to see how his money was being spent, "a lot of it would just make him furious."

## Nathan Cummings Foundation

Nathan Cummings, owner of a giant food firm that later became the well-known Sara Lee Corporation, was a Jewish immigrant who established his charitable foundation in 1949 by declaring, "we must contribute to worthy causes, thus sharing our good fortune with those less fortunate than we are." Big recipients were mainstream groups and particularly universities, hospitals, medical centers and Israel.

After Cummings' death in 1985, his $200 million estate was bequeathed to the foundation and his children were left with the task of continuing his charitable giving. This planted the seed for a *coup d'etat*— where yet another charity would turn to the dark side of liberalism. The children wanted a new vision and mission, and the grandchildren persuaded their skeptical parents to hire a liberal consultant familiar with philanthropy. Everything went downhill from there.

While the Cummings Foundation still gives to mainstream arts groups, a check of its federal tax 990 forms reveals that the list of grantees that support everything from "multiculturalism" to anti-capital punishment crusades has ballooned. Presided over by grandson James K. Cummings, the foundation his grandfather established now ploughs big bucks into the Council on Foreign Relations and left-wing foundations, including Tides (over $275,000 in 2004), and is a faithful annual supporter of the Council on Foundations ($35,000 in 2004). It invests in well-known organizations ranging from the American Civil Liberties Union and the Sierra Club to obscure outfits like the New York Lesbian and Gay Experimental Film Festival. It gave Greenpeace $150,000 in 2004 and even handed $35,000 that year to the pro-Communist National Lawyers Guild.

73

In 2004, the foundation's assets were $447.5 million; grants awarded that year totaled $19.1 million.

## Open Society Institute

"The main obstacle to a stable and just world is the United States," writes the founder of this institute. If the "old-timer" Ford Foundation rates as the prime funder and friend of leftists, this billionaire "Dr. Evil" is emerging as "No. 2 and trying harder." George Soros' promotion of left-wing and anti-American causes merits a book in itself.

Born of Jewish parents in Hungary, Soros arrived on Wall Street in 1956 and soon became known as a savvy financial manager and investor by clients of his Quantum Fund. Financial publications credit Soros as one of the creators of the risky "hedge fund." Author Lowell Pointe notes that in 1992 the global high-roller "wagered $10 billion that by concerted attack he could devalue the British pound." Pointe writes "he won," and ended up with "at least $1.1 billion in profit in a single day, and ever since has been called 'the man who broke the Bank of England.'" One goal was to strike a blow against British Prime Minister John Major's Conservative government, and the devaluation helped topple it from power.

Other questionable Soros dealings caused economic collapse in Southeast Asia in 1997, leading Malaysian officials to specifically blame him. Five years later a French court declared him guilty of insider trading and fined him 2.2 million Euros ($2 million— a slap on the wrist to this billionaire.)

In 1979 Soros founded the Open Society Institute (OSI), the first of his several foundations. Among board members are Lani Guiner, a radical Democrat from the Clinton era who espouses racial quotas, and Bill Moyers, a prominent liberal journalist. Soros' apparent motivation— and that of OSI— is hatred of Christianity and that "right-wingers" and "fascists" must be counterbalanced by a more powerful left. His 1998 book *The Crisis of Global Capitalism: Open*

*Society Endangered* calls for government control over "amoral" capitalist corporations.

OSI assets totaled over $175 million in 2001 and, after the al Qaeda attacks on America, it channeled funding to anti-American Muslims. One favorite is the so-called American-Arab Anti-Discrimination Committee Research Institute that defends Palestinian suicide bombers. The Institute, through its communications guru Hussein Ibish, defends the bombers so long as they don't target "civilians." This group also defends one-time Florida professor Sami al-Arian, deported for terrorist links.

Soros' philanthropic work in Russia and Europe is extensive. One project involved linking Russian universities to the Internet. He created foundations targeting specific countries for different missions, especially for education and public health projects. His sympathy for radical Islamists was shown by support for Kosovo guerrillas— and their goal of an independent Muslim state— in their war against the Christian Serbs. OSI opened a branch office in Pristina, for example, after the NATO occupation of Kosovo. Researcher Michel Chossudovsky of the Center for Research on Globalization notes a Soros foundation paper urging that mineral rights owned by the Serbs be seized by NATO "as quickly as possible" for the Kosovars and their international speculator and banker friends. Chossudovsky's research also found the Kosovo Foundation for an Open Society supplied "targeted support" grants for local governments— all controlled by racist Muslim Kosovars busy ethnically cleansing the province of Serbs.

Black Muslims are also beloved by the OSI. In 2001 it gave $65,000 to the Marxist-oriented Malcolm X Grassroots Movement— a black gangster counterpart to the white Aryan Nations group. It extremist agenda includes establishing a black "homeland" in the American South— stretching from Louisiana to South Carolina— and its website lauds numerous black Muslims who have killed policemen. Soros foundations give specifically to the NAACP Legal Defense and Education Fund for defending anti-white extremists, most of them police killers. (Soros apparently equates the police with "fascists.") OSI, along with the Ford and MacArthur foundations, further supports The Sentencing Project which advocates voting rights for felons. In 2002 OSI specifically gave the Tides Foundation $400,000 for a project to "re-enfranchise felons."

Soros continually gives to the pro-Communist National Lawyers Guild ($50,000 one recent year) and a massive OSI donation launched The Center for the Study of Constitutional Rights (CCR). He awarded $160,000 (along with the Ford Foundation) to that group in recent years to help defend Communists and radical Muslims.

Soros' vision of achieving "world peace" makes the United Nations a favorite, including the left-leaning United Nations Correspondents Association. Eric Shawn in *The U.N. Exposed* documents that OSI, Ted Turner's United Nations Foundation and the Rockefeller Foundation unethically give money to supposedly objective journalists covering the world body, and fund journalism "prizes" for the Correspondents' Association. The Soros-funded People for the American Way created a left-wing "peace movement" during the Bush administration, spawning groups like the radical International ANSWER and a separate group the United for Peace and Justice, whose pro-Communist leader Leslie Cagan extols Cuban tyrant Fidel Castro.

The billionaire is perhaps best known for his vocal hatred of President George W. Bush, who he compares to Nazi *fuehrer* Adolf Hitler. Soros pledged to raise $75 million to defeat Bush for re-election in 2004, and personally donated a third of that to anti-Bush groups. Five million went to MoveOn.org, which produced ads comparing Bush to Hitler. Ten million went to a Democratic Party get-out-the-vote campaign called America Coming Together (ACT). Ellen Malcolm, founder of the pro-abortion group EMILY's List, was ACT president and its board included the Sierra's Club's Carl Pope and Cecile Richards, a former aide to U.S. House Democrat leader Rep. Nancy Pelosi, D-Ca.

Aside from supporting extreme groups and causes, Soros's deep pockets extend to dozens of "mainstream" ultraliberal groups ranging from the American Civil Liberties Union (millions in recent years) to feminist groups like the National Organization for Women, the Feminist Majority and NARAL Pro Choice America. The president of OSI, in fact, is Aryeh Neier, the 15-year one-time national ACLU director.

Soros also made headlines by targeting $50 million to a variety of pro-illegal alien and open-door advocacy groups, including the National Immigration Forum and the ACLU, specifically to agitate for open door immigration policies. The Million Mom March in 2002, a huge anti-gun rally, was primarily funded by Soros. And he gives freely to other foundations, such as grants to the Tides Foundation/Center of over $13 million between 1997 and 2003. The list of this Santa Claus to the left will no doubt grow longer in coming years.

## Pew Charitable Trusts

Like John D. MacArthur, founder Joseph N. Pew and his immediate heirs were conservatives. Pew's trusts, comprised of seven individual funds founded between 1948 and 1979 by Joseph Pew and his children, primarily funded patriotic, religious and pro-business organizations and projects. In the early decades the trusts performed fine humanitarian work. But, as with MacArthur, heirs who tried to follow the founder's philosophy lost legal control to leftists and feminists.

DiscovertheNetworks.org found that in 2003 the Philadelphia-based PCT had $4.1 billion in assets, and committed more than $143 million to 151 non-profit organizations. In 2004 it made the transition from a private foundation to an independent public charity, thus making it easier to lobby Congress and state legislatures on the alleged global warming threat.

Consider part of Pew's immature and saccharine mission statement:

> *The major social and political battlefields since*
> *World War II— the civil rights, anti-Vietnam War,*
> *women's, anti-nuclear and environment movements—*

*all depended on the idealism, the ideas and action of the young. In today's current debates over the environment, health care and education, the viewpoints of youth need to be essential voices in making the* proper *policy decisions.* (Emphasis mine.)

The takeover of these trusts is graphically recounted by DiscovertheNetworks.org:

> *Rebecca Rimel, who presently heads the foundation, began her career in 1983 as the health program manager. She became executive director in 1998 and ascended to the positions of president and chief executive officer of the board in 1994 when her mentor, neurosurgeon Thomas W. Langfitt, retired. It was Langfitt who changed the cultural direction of the foundation by transforming a rich, old-fashioned family philanthropy into his idea of a modern, left-wing foundation. In the late 1980s he engineered a complete makeover of the program staff and a redirection of Pew's grant–making priorities... Notably, the foundation's entire executive office is run exclusively by women.*

Pew, like other big foundations, seeks to "understand" Islam. There's nothing wrong with that *per se,* but— as evidenced by Rimel's speeches and by papers posted on the Pew website— there is an underlying politically correct, blame–America theme. Its researchers release all too many inane surveys like one indicating that in Jordan, Morocco and Pakistan "the public supports suicide bombings in Iraq, and Osama bin Laden is still far more popular than President Bush in those three countries." Its 2004 Pew Global Attitudes Project, which involved polling people in the U.S. and eight foreign countries, was headed by former Secretary of State Madeleine Albright. She, of course, served in a Clinton administration that underestimated Islamic terrorism and failed to curb or kill bin Laden in the 1990s.

The Pew Hispanic Center cranks out many a poll. Yet, as with any survey, the wording is key— so when the Pew "spin" is affixed on queries the results often end up sympathetic to illegal aliens in general and for their amnesty or coddling in particular. One Pew writer on its website seems to delight in stating that the U.S. is now a "major Spanish speaking country."

It's ironic that while Pew supports a number of militantly anti-corporate and anti-capitalist organizations (including what CEO Rimel admiringly calls "raging environmentalist" groups) it simultaneously holds multi-million investments in big corporations. It invests in ExxonMobil, for example, while funding groups that routinely attack that company on its environmental record and for countering global warming propaganda.

Former Clinton administration official Eileen Claussen is president of the Pew Center on Global Climate Change and its Environmental Program. *Foundation Watch* characterizes it as a huge ATM that funds climate change campaigns. The newsletter gives a few examples:

- $29 million from 1995-2002 to the Earthjustice Legal Defense Fund (formerly the Sierra Club Legal Defense Fund) which files numerous lawsuits involving industrial emissions.

- $11.5 million from 1991-2000 to the Natural Resources Defense Council and $6.3 million during 1990-2000 to Environmental Defense, two global warming opponents.

- $24 million from 1998 to 2002 to Strategies for the Global Environment, parent corporation of the Pew Center on Global Climate Change.

- $2.9 million from 1992 to 2002 to the Union of Concerned Scientists, a big fossil fuel critic.

Pew and a number of grant recipients are crusaders for the severe energy cuts mandated by 1) the 1992 United Nations Framework Convention on Climate Change, which critics charge would cripple the Western industrial world; and 2) the Kyoto Protocol that targets carbon dioxide as the chief greenhouse gas that supposedly causes world temperatures to rise. (Kyoto applies to the U.S. but exempts "developing" countries like China and India that are big polluters.)

Pew's National Environmental Trust once sponsored, in the words of *The National Journal,* a "bare knuckles paid media campaign" to defeat a congressional deregulation bill— typical of its decades-long lobbying for virtually every costly climate change legislation imaginable. Heir Howard Pew's old foundation paid for ads claiming Congress is "bedding down with corporate polluters," which led *Philanthropy Roundtable* to note say "he built the fortune that became the Pew trusts by being precisely the kind of person vilified in those ads."

## Rockefeller Foundation & Rockefeller Brothers Fund

Rockefeller family money over the 20th century has been spent on a variety of fine philanthropic causes. At the same time the late Nelson Rockefeller, the longtime New York governor and vice president, along with his band of brothers, pumped enormous sums into not just left-wing and but anti-American venues that have affected U.S. culture and world affairs.

The Rockefeller Foundation, brainchild of patriarch and industrialist John D., emerged after the national income tax law in 1913. It made sense to form a foundation for "tax protection" as well as to promote a political and social worldview.

An early tip-off of the Rockefeller worldview was the funding of the notorious Institute of Pacific Relations, founded in 1925. It began as an association of national councils that would coordinate research, publications and conferences, overseen by an international body headquartered in New York City. By 1950 it included national councils from the United States (the American Institute of Pacific Relations), Canada, Great Britain, France, a smattering of other Western nations and some Asian countries. Between 1931 and 1939, the Soviet Union under tyrant Joseph Stalin had a member-council.

Author Francis X. Gannon notes that from 1925 until 1950 the IPR received 77 percent of its finances from American foundations and the AIPR. In turn, the AIPR received 50 percent of its support from Rockefeller and Carnegie entities.

The research and discussion that originally marked the IPR evolved into open promotion of Communist objectives. If that sounds harsh, consider that the organization was the target of a wide-ranging U.S. Senate committee probe which uncovered IPR members' assistance to the Communist intelligence network. One prominent member of this network was convicted perjurer and Soviet spy Alger Hiss. Alfred Kohlberg, a disgruntled AIPR official, tipped off Senate investigators after discovering numerous IPR publications parroting the Soviet and Chinese Communist propaganda line. Seven years after Kohlberg blew the whistle, the Senate Internal Security Subcommittee concluded:

> *A small core of officials and staff members carried the main burden of IPR activities and directed its administration and policies. Members of the small core of officials and staff members were either Communist or pro-Communist.*

The panel couldn't prove the funders knew of IPR's "inner workings"— yet the Rockefellers never apologized for supporting an organization that clearly undermined our side during the Cold War. The foundation has also never been apologetic for its massive funding, since 1927, of the Council on Foreign Relations— mentioned in the previous chapter for its internationalism at the expense of American sovereignty. Former Ambassador John Kenneth Galbraith once bragged that "it is as much of the ruling establishment" as is the State Department. To quote Gannon:

*Upon the cessation of World War II, it became evident that the CFR was determined in its role as The Ruling Establishment to brook no interference in its campaign to stamp the United States with its brand of modern liberalism and its facets of statism and internationalism.*

There is a tremendous body of evidence, much of it recorded in the CFR publication *Foreign Affairs,* revealing an array of American members to be incredibly soft on communism, as well as being reliable supporters of the United Nations and world government. American contributors over the years included Nelson and David Rockefeller (naturally), Edward House, former President Franklin Roosevelt (a CFR favorite), Paul Hoffman (of the Ford Foundation), Dean Acheson, Dean Rusk, Adlai Stevenson, former President John F. Kennedy and security risk J. Robert Oppenheimer.

Not every *Foreign Affairs* contributor or CFR member, of course, seeks to replace the U.S. Constitution with a one-world government. Some like to debate or write about world issues within the privacy of this elite establishment. Conservative scribe William F. Buckley Jr. is one such member. Rusk, who served as President Lyndon Johnson's secretary of state and was a Rockefeller Foundation president, told the University of Georgia's Demosthenian Society he especially savored "off-the-record" CFR gatherings.

The CFR is a large part of the Rockefeller legacy. So, too, is the foundation's massive funding in the 1940s and '50s of Alfred Kinsey's flawed sex studies and books that impact today's culture and law (covered in chapter seven). But there's far more.

The Rockefeller Brothers Fund (RBF)— founded in 1940 as a vehicle through which John D.'s sons and daughter could disseminate advice— is controlled by third, fourth and fifth generation Rockefellers. It promotes "multiculturalism," thus often aiding America's enemies. Its "Peace and Security Program" fosters, in its words, "greater understanding between Muslim and Western societies." Left unaddressed is the radical Islamic movement that spreads terrorism in an effort to destroy non-Muslim civilization.

RBF's "Peace and Security Program" places responsibility for international disharmony squarely on the United States. "At the start of the 21$^{st}$ century and in the wake of Sept. 11, 2001," says the PSP, "there exists a pressing need to examine the content, style and tone of the U.S. global engagement and to ensure that they reflect an understanding of the reality and implications of increasing global independence."

Another program is "The Distinguished Speakers Series" hosted by the American Iranian Council (AIC), an agent of Iran which, according to the U.S. State Department, is the world's top funder of state-sponsored terrorism. In 2004 the AIC had no shame in presenting an anti-American lecture by Iran's Ambassador to the U.N. Javad Zarif without an opposing point of view. DiscovertheNetworks.org found:

> *The AIC is a lobbying group that has consistently supported lifting U.S. sanctions on Iran and accommodating the repressive, fundamentalist Tehran regime. It is also a heavy backer of the Democratic Party, and seeks to bring about a normalization of the relationship between the U.S. and radical mullahs of Iran.*

Author Ron Arnold of the Center for Defense of Free Enterprise emphasizes that the Rockefeller Family Fund (along with other foundations) subsidizes an ongoing smear campaign against the ExxonMobil Company, headed by non-leftists who dare to fight back against the foundations' "invisible government" and who have funded think tanks questioning the Al Gores of the world on climate change. The Rockefeller anti-ExxonMobil money was funneled through an outfit called the Environmental Integrity Project.

Big Rockefeller bucks flow to Greenpeace, Environmental Media Services, the Friends of the Earth, the Natural Resources Defense Council, the Environmental Defense Fund, the Sierra Club, the Rainforest Action Network, the World Resources Institute, the Earth Island Institute, the Environmental Working Group, the Izaak Walton League, the Open Space Institute, the Conservation Law Foundation, U.S. Public Interest Research Group, the Wilderness

Society, the Worldwatch Institute, the Union of Concerned Scientists, Ozone Action, the Pacific Rivers Council, the Rainforest Alliance, the National Wildlife Federation, the Pesticide Action Network, the League of Conservation Voters, the Waterkeeper Alliance and additional alarmists who battle for bigger government and more regulatory burdens on business.

Operating out of the RBF's Madison Avenue offices is the Environmental Grantmakers Association, which funds a wide array of radicalism among evangelical churches (and is featured in chapter six).

Other "politically correct" RBF grant recipients include the Puerto Rican Legal Defense and Education Fund, the Gay Men's Health Crisis, The Sentencing Project, The Lawyer's Committee for Human Rights, Amnesty International, The Third World Network, the United Nations Foundation and the United Nations Association of the United States. It also funded the now-defunct TechRocks headed by David's son Richard Rockefeller, which provided high-tech support to radical anti-corporate non-profits.

As of 2004, the combined assets of the RBF, the Foundation and the Rockefeller Family Fund totaled $3.5 billion.

## William and Flora Hewlett Foundation

Founded by William R. Hewlett (of Hewlett-Packard Co. fame) and his wife in 1966 to "promote the well-being of humanity," it is one of the nation's largest foundations. Hewlett died in 2001 and willed his foundation over $5 billion. In 2004 alone it awarded more than $268,427,895 in grants.

The Hewlett Foundation is a proud member of the Peace and Security Funders, a loose group of private and public foundations that underwrite anti-Iraq war and environmentalist causes. Among these are the Natural Resources Defense Council and others featured in the next chapter.

84

One of its few worthwhile grantmaking areas involves what Hewlett's website titles "The U.S.-Latin America Relations Program." It heavily funds "air quality" projects particularly in Mexican cities but throughout Latin America.

Hewlett is known for an ongoing love affair with feminist and pro-abortion groups. Consider just these recipients among dozens listed on its federal tax 990 forms: Ms. Foundation for Women, Global Fund for Women, Reproductive Health Technologies Project, National Partnership for Women and Families, National Latina Institute for Reproductive Health, National Family Planning and Reproductive Health Association, Medical Students for Choice, Gender and Rights and the Center for Development and Population Activities. During 2003-2005 it gave over $2 million to the Center for Reproductive Rights, a legal advocacy organization that works to impose abortion on demand.

One "sex education" recipient— the Sexuality Information and Education Council of the United States— is notorious for promoting permissiveness and even incest. (SIECUS is covered more extensively in chapter seven.) Hewlett also invests with other foundations to grow the pro-abortion, New York-based Alan Guttmacher Institute.

Hewlett dotes over the American Civil Liberties Union and, to assist in erasing U.S. borders and change the U.S. into a multicultural nation, the foundation annually shovels money to the Mexican American Legal Defense and Education Fund as well as to numerous local pro-illegal immigrant projects typified by one at City University of New York that assists aliens to melt into society.

One of its favorite charities, too, is the fossil fuel-hating, San Francisco-based Energy Foundation, mentioned in the MacArthur Foundation section.

A recognizable and surprisingly Republican name on the Hewlett board is Condoleeza Rice, Secretary of State in the Bush administration.

# Schumann Foundation

A relative newcomer funding the respectable and disreputable left is the Florence and John Schumann Foundation, now known as the Schumann Center for Media and Democracy. Florence's father was a founder of IBM, and husband John amassed General Motors money during his career. Enjoying tax-exempt status since 1966 and chaired by son Robert Schumann, its assets in 2001 topped $60.9 million. But it was when journalist Bill Moyers became president that Schumann swerved far to portside.

Author Ben Johnson cites Moyers' funding of a once-obscure journal, *The American Prospect*, that he wanted as a counterbalance to a major conservative publication:

> *Moyers turned loose the foundation's spigots and flooded TAP with pledges of nearly $11 million. It was a $5.5 million grant in 1999 that transformed TAP from an academic journal to a biweekly newsstand publication meant to rival National Review. Although Schumann money conferred respectability upon this publication, TAP maintains connections to the radical left. The editor-at-large, Harold Meyerson, is a vice chair of the Democratic Socialists of America. TAP founders include Robert Kuttner and diminutive Clinton Labor Secretary Robert Reich.*

DiscovertheNetworks.org reports it was Schumann money that helped launch the virulently left-wing website TomPaine.com, and funded anti-American actor Sean Penn's first propaganda trip to Baghdad before the Iraq war. One example of the foundation's "anti-war" activity comes from The Florence Fund headed by Moyers' son John. It is a part of the Schumann enterprise. It contributed to a full-page *New York Times* ad to promote the "Win Without War" anti-Iraq war coalition. The unethical Moyers interviewed on his Public Broadcasting Service TV program two "Win Without War" officials without ever disclosing his tie to the guests.

During interviews with liberal journalists at the National Press Club bar in Washington, D.C., it became evident to this author that their new hero is The Schumann Center for Media and Democracy. It has emerged as a huge crutch for leftist journalists.

Its money funds the so-called Institute for Public Accuracy, headed by leftist Norman Solomon, and Citizen Action. Citizen Action, by the way, remains tainted since the late 1990s because of participation in an illegal money laundering scandal also involving the AFL-CIO, the Democratic Party and Clinton re-election campaign officials.

## Tides Foundation & Tides Center

The San-Francisco-based Tides Foundation, founded in 1976 by California activist Drummond Pike, says it donates to "strengthen community-based organizations and the progressive movement"— a trendy name for the hard left. It established three for-profit media enterprises and underwrote them by donating to Tides (which in turn kicked money back to the Pew media companies). This setup allows the "charity" to channel money from wealthy donors to left-wing radicals without the donors being publicly associated with any direct giving. In addition to funding a wide range of environmental action groups, it donates to many an ultraliberal cause ranging from gun control to gay, lesbian, bisexual and transgender advocacy. This is underwritten, in large measure, by the Pew Charitable Trusts.

Tides gives to the National Lawyers Guild, that onetime legal bulwark of the Communist Party which now defends anti-war groups and radical Islamists. Its "9/11 Fund" was replaced by a "Democratic Justice Fund," which received over $7 million in recent years by George Soros' Open Society Institute. Tides wades deeper into the anti-war fever swamp with its Institute for Global Communications, a provider of web assistance to radicals. The IGC website actually "recommends" linked sites such as the International Action Center controlled by Ramsey Clark, the late Saddam Hussein's lawyer and longtime defender of America's enemies. Tides further funds the Council for American Islamic Relations (CAIR), a group frequently on the wrong side in America's war on terror and which opposes so-called "racial profiling" of Muslims at the border or on airplanes.

Its federal tax 990 forms also indicate that Greenpeace and virtually all the radical environmental groups listed in the next chapter are recipients of Tides largesse.

The Tides Center, founded in 1979, is best described by DiscovertheNetworks.org as "a legal firewall insulating the Tides Foundation from legal action taken by people harmed by Tides Foundation-funded environmental and animal-rights groups and projects. This could include, for instance, farmers or loggers who are put out of business by such groups."

Additionally, the Tides Center manages the foundation's array of 200-plus left-wing projects. Net assets of the Tides Foundation totaled $144.2 million in 2004; the Center totaled $36.6 million. In terms of grants awarded, the foundation doled out $74.1 million in 2004; the Center $10 million during the same year.

## Turner Foundation

The Atlanta, Ga.-based Turner Foundation is controlled by "mouth of the South" and Cable News Network founder Ted Turner, who was once married to left-wing actress Jane Fonda. It has funded some excellent conservation, habitat preservation and other nature projects since its founding in 1990. Unfortunately, grantmaking tilts far to the left.

The founder once cynically proclaimed, according to the July 2003 NewsMax.com: "If there is a God, He is not doing a good job of protecting the earth. He has kind of checked out." That may explain the following grants in the environmental arena:

- $19.2 million to the League of Conservation Voters (2001-2002)
- $4.1 million to the Natural Resources Defense Council (1993-2002)

- $3.4 million to the National Wildlife Federation (1994-2002)
- $1.9 million to the Tides Foundation/Center (1994-2002)
- $1.3 million to Greenpeace (1996-2001)
- $1.2 million to the Sierra Club (1993-2002)
- $985,000 to the U.S. Public Interest Research Group (1994-2002)
- $727,000 to the Union of Concerned Scientists (1994-2002)
- $500,000 to the Rainforest Action Network (1994-2001)
- $351,000 to the Wilderness Society (1994-2002)

Activities and projects of all these radical groups are documented in the next chapter.

Affiliated organizations listed on the Turner Foundation website are the United Nations Foundation, the Nuclear Threat Initiative, the Better World Fund (UN-oriented) and the Captain Planet Foundation. The best charitable work is done by the Captain Planet Foundation, which gets young students in the U.S. and foreign countries involved in nature appreciation and conservation— although that is obscured by publicity generated by Turner's periodic and erratic pro-United Nations, anti-Christian rhetoric.

The anti-Christian insults, though, don't bother the money-hungry, left-wing National Council of Churches. In the 2004-2005 fiscal year, the NCC received $37,000 from the UN Foundation and Better World Fund for "ecojustice" projects and promotion of the Kyoto treaty.

Turner's environmental concerns, though, have limitations. *Fortune* in 2003 reported that "this past spring there was a tussle over his decision to accelerate natural gas drilling on his largest property, his 580,000-acre Vermejo Park ranch in New Mexico. Beau Turner, who manages the properties' wildlife, vehemently opposed the drilling, but his father cut a deal with the rights holder, El Paso Corp., for an enhanced royalty."

His son challenged his father: "Dad, if you weren't in these financial straits, would you be doing this? He told me no," Turner told the magazine, "I wouldn't have done it if not for the decline of the stock."

Turner Foundation assets in recent years have hovered around $148 million.

## A few upstarts to watch

Keep an eye on the following leftist foundations poised to grow larger either in assets or influence in coming years:

The William J. Clinton Foundation, founded by the former president; the Barbara Streisand Foundation, controlled by the popular actress who supports liberal candidates and causes; the older Wilburforce, Bauman and Surdna foundations, especially active in the environmental arena ("Surdna spelled backwards is "Andrus," after founder John Andrus); the Blue Moon Fund, presently enraptured in funding myriad projects in Communist China.

The David Geffen Foundation, sugar daddy to various homosexual organizations and projects, could also expand its horizons and emerge as a far more diversified player.

# FUNDING RADICAL ENVIRONMENTALISTS
## CHAPTER V

*"All technology should be assumed guilty until proven innocent." – The late Sierra Club executive director David Brower.*

The fable writer Aesop observed, "We often give our enemies the means of our own destruction." Nowhere is this seen so clearly than in corporate America, where charitable foundations established by entrepreneurs provide tens of millions of dollars a year to radicals bent on tearing down a free enterprise system which has created the economic engine that is the envy of the world.

Why do so many corporations and foundations give to those who would destroy the very system that created their wealth?

Promoting feel-good "environmental" and "global warming" research and campaigns boost foundations' donations. That fuels the "invisible government" agenda of more government regulation, more taxation and even ultimate United Nations control over land and sea resources. Appearing to be "green" can be a good public relations spin. As for corporations, another explanation is that all too many donate to radical groups in order to protect themselves against future waves of costly, image-shattering litigation.

It was in 2002 when the Rev. Jesse Jackson's Rainbow/PUSH Coalition and affiliated groups came under fire for soliciting tax-deductible contributions from corporations against whom he promised to "campaign" on alleged employment diversity issues. Many radical environmental groups take the same approach to corporate blackmail.

The environmental movement has achieved important public health and conservation victories, just as the civil rights movement that gave rise to Jackson's career achieved much needed legal guarantees for Americans of all races. Yet, in order to foster the thriving "victim" industry, the dollar-hungry mouths of radical environmentalists rely on scare tactics and threats of public relations and litigation terror to survive and grow.

"Fear is a great motivator" to arouse public action, Hollywood global warming activist Laurie David cynically proclaims. A prime fear-monger, previously noted, is the heavily foundation-backed Greenpeace. (It was co-founder Patrick Moore who left it for "abandoning science and logic.") Then there are countless Greenpeace copycats honey-combed with leftists. The following are snapshots of the influential ones listed in alphabetical order:

## Defenders of Wildlife

This innocent-sounding Washington-based group, founded in 1947, is a militant foe of America's war on terrorism, highlighted by its website accusations that the Defense Department and Department of Homeland Security are sacrificing our natural heritage at the expense of national security. The Defenders oppose oil exploration in the Arctic National Wildlife Refuge in Alaska, and are more radical than most other groups in how they propose restricting huge tracts of public land. If you check its website, ranchers are an enemy as well as anyone who dares advocate the use of recreational vehicles on public land.

The Defenders are also open border advocates who undermine the U.S. Border Patrol's work in policing the 2,000-mile U.S.-Mexican boundary to combat human, drug and weapons trafficking. DOW official Jamie Rappaport Clark complains, "The Border Patrol's blanket requests for unlimited motorized access to protected parks, monuments and wilderness areas are being made behind closed doors without any opportunity for public involvement." In 2003 the organization attacked the Department of Defense for seeking exemption from restrictive environmental policies on the border so the military could better monitor illegal immigrants, including possible foreign terrorist infiltration.

The Defenders rail against construction of fences, lighting and other barriers to deter illegal immigration on our southwestern border. DOW, the Sierra Club and Audubon Society sued the Immigration and Naturalization Service in 1998 claiming the building of such barriers in Arizona "would have ended any hope for further cross-border movement by jaguars, ocelots and a host of other border species."

The open borders Turner Foundation delights in funding DOW to the tune of over $1 million since 1997— precisely because it is a thorn on the side of immigration control using the guise of "environmentalism." Other supporters are the Bullit Foundation, the Bauman Family Foundation, the David and Lucille Packard Foundation and the Barbra Streisand Foundation.

## Environmentalists Against War

Berkeley, California, home of many on the loony left, is the birthplace of this hodgepodge of environmental crazies and anti-war warriors. Peter Drekmeier, China Brotsky, Josh Karliner and Gar Smith established Environmentalists Against War to protest the U.S.-led overthrow of Iraq dictator Saddam Hussein and, as its website says, to oppose "domestic attacks on immigrants." Smith believes American dependency on foreign oil is somehow responsible for the Sept. 11 terror attacks against America, and he actually recommends that the U.S. "give up its position as the world's reigning superpower."

On May 1, 2003 EAW published "Ten Reasons Environmentalists Oppose the Attack on Iraq." Reflect on some of the sophomoric "reasons":

- The attack on Iraq could kill thousands of people. Most of the people killed would be innocent civilians.
- War destroys human settlements and native habitats. War destroys wildlife and contaminates the land, air and water. The damage can last for generations.
- U.S. cluster bombs ... and weapons made with depleted uranium are indiscriminate weapons of mass destruction.
- Bombs pollute, poisoning the land with unexploded shells and toxic chemicals ...
- Fighting a war for oil is ultimately self-defeating.

This outfit never mentions Saddam's bombing and gassing of innocent civilians. Nor could this author find that any of its writings note, let alone condemn, Saddam's burning of Kuwaiti oil fields when he invaded that country in 1991. Now *that* was an environmental catastrophe. The EAW only targets the U.S. for condemnation.

EAW conducts sit-ins and teach-ins and has no problem marching or proselytizing alongside Communist counterparts. It was an endorser of the "Books Not Bombs" protest in 2003 urging American students to strike against the Iraq war, joining other endorsers like the pro-Castroite Global Exchange and the Young Communist League.

DiscovertheNetworks.org uncovered the fact that EAW's registration form for a 2003 teach-in directed that checks be written to "Environmentalists Against War/Tides Center." That's because EAW founder Brotsky serves as special projects director for the Tides Foundation and Center.

# Environmental Working Group

The incredible dishonesty of the Washington-based EWG is cited in the first chapter. Now consider— again quoting from DiscovertheNetworks.org— the dynamos driving it. Board member David Fenton "worked with the Natural Resources Defense Council to manufacture the 1989 Alar pesticide scare... and now has put his efforts into the Hollywood-dominated 'Win Without War,' which opposes the Bush administration's effort to keep terrorists and madmen in check." Fenton was a '60s radical, a photographer for the Weatherman terrorist group, and journalist for *Liberation News*. Other influential EWG players include Michael Casey, 1992 press secretary for the Clinton-Gore campaign, and Bill Walker, a Greenpeace veteran and head of EWG's Oakland office. There's also Kelsey Wirth, treasurer of EWG and daughter of former Colorado senator Tim Wirth, now head of Ted Turner's United Nations Foundation."

In spite of the bad press it has received, its website indicates EWG plugs away against the use of all pesticides. Yet in the arena of banning the chemical spray DDT, EWG is not only meeting resistance from conservatives but from intellectually honest liberals. Liberal Alexander Gourevich, writing in *The Washington Monthly*, says "when it comes to the kinds of uses once permitted in the United States and abroad, there's simply no solid scientific evidence that exposure to DDT causes cancer or is otherwise harmful to human beings. Not a single study linking DDT exposure to human toxicity has ever been replicated." Malcolm Gladwell, writing in the *New Yorker,* reminds readers that "between 1945 and 1965, DDT saved millions— even tens of millions of lives around the world" when it came to fighting disease.

The Ford Foundation still believes in the EWG, giving over $500,000 since 1996, as well as the Pew Charitable Trusts (also $500,000-plus). They are joined by the Rockefeller Family Fund, the Heinz Family Fund and the Turner Foundation.

# Friends of the Earth

A review of its website reveals the Washington-based Friends of the Earth (FOE) to be a consistent enemy of both corporate America and domestic energy independence. In the words of writer Michael Berliner, its agenda seeks:

> ... *not clean air and clean water, (but) rather ... the demolition of technological/industrial civilization. (Radical) environmentalism's goal is not the advancement of human health, human happiness and human life; rather it is a subhuman world where 'nature' is worshipped like the totem of some primitive religion ... environmentalists have made 'development' an evil word. They inhibit or prohibit the development of Alaskan oil, off-shore drilling, nuclear power— and every other practical form of energy. Housing, commerce and jobs are sacrificed to spotted owls and snail darters. Medical research is sacrificed to the 'rights' of mice. Logging is sacrificed to the 'rights' of trees. No instance of the progress that brought man out of the cave is safe ...*

FOE's record includes fighting to keep millions of acres off-limits to energy exploration in Alaska and elsewhere. It joined the campaign, during the Clinton administration, to remove 1.7 million acres in Utah from reasonable gas and oil exploration.

The Friends played dirty when it came to blocking the Small Business Administration from lending to companies not in tune with its agenda. In 2003 the FOE won a legal settlement to prevent the SBA from what the plaintiffs called "fueling urban sprawl." The SBA had provided approximately $45 million for construction and expansion of various businesses, but FOE painted with a broad brush by arguing that such developments lead to more pollution. (In fact, air and water are cleaner in the last 25 years according to Environmental Protection Agency Air Quality and Emissions Trends Reports.)

In 2003 FOE filed another lawsuit to force the EPA to further "regulate carbon dioxide and other greenhouse gases as air pollutants and contributors to global warming." Furthermore, it joined a post-Sept. 11, 2001 campaign opposing U.S. interventions in Afghanistan and Iraq. It is a member of the United for Peace and Justice anti-war coalition, and endorses the "Ten Reasons Environmentalists Oppose an Attack on Iraq."

Friends get help from their friends, receiving over $7 million in foundation grants from 1994-2004. Donors include the Charles Stewart Mott Foundation, the W. Alton Jones Fund (now called the Blue Moon Fund), the Pew Charitable Trusts; the MacArthur Foundation, the Ford Foundation and the Turner Foundation.

## Global Resource Action Center for the Environment

"Factory farming" and nuclear disarmament are the main issues motivating this New York City-based non-profit founded in 1996 by wealthy animal rights and anti-nuclear activist Helaine Lerner.

Everybody waxes nostalgic for the American "family farm," but large agribusiness operations have basically replaced them. So what better villain than so-called "factory farms"? GRACE president Alice Slater in January 2004 said, "Factory farms pose enormous health threats, not only within rural communities, but in the supermarket where the public is at risk of eating contaminated meat raised with unsustainable practices." Slater claims "factory farms" can't or won't meet acceptable health standards, and thus foster diseases like mad cow disease. Unfortunately for Slater, there is little evidence any of this is true. A 2001 foot-and-mouth disease outbreak in Great Britain, for example, originated from a small family farm. GRACE simply invokes the "fear" message against what it describes as uncaring capitalists who operate large farming concerns.

GRACE has another obsession. Its website notes it is a member of the "Abolition 2000" coalition which pledges to eliminate nuclear weapons and provide "technical support to grassroots activists living in the shadow of the U.S. nuclear weapons complex." It opposes any

97

U.S. nuclear missile defense and belongs to the Peace and Security Funders, a network of grant-making operations which underwrite anti-war and environmental causes.

GRACE is a signatory to an April 2001 petition opposing further development of all nuclear technology. Interestingly, this militant stand is now being critiqued by mainstream liberals— including newspaper editorial writers— who are coming to realize the need for clean, safe and cheap nuclear power in order to keep their home light bulbs burning and their furnaces humming.

By opposing all "radioactive contamination," GRACE criticizes irradiation as a food treatment process. This flies in the face of many studies, including those by the Atlanta-based Centers for Disease Control, showing that irradiation effectively removes organic contaminants from food and thereby increases its shelf-life.

Since 2000 GRACE has received millions from founder Lerner's foundations. It also maintains a front group, the tax-exempt GRACE Public Fund, which tries to influence Capitol Hill legislation.

## Izaak Walton League

The League began in 1922 as a benign conservation group focusing on soil and stream pollution, and urging responsible education and public policy to combat it. In recent years, the League has morphed into a villain that revels in shaking down corporate America and even the federal government.

Headquartered in Gaithersburg, Md., and named after a medieval English conservationist, it is one of the oldest conservation organizations and claims 50,000 members. Now its website pushes U.S. nuclear disarmament, lobbies against ranching and opposes the use of recreational motorized vehicles. When President George W. Bush in 2003 asked Congress to pass the "Healthy Forest Initiative" designed to thin out forests and dense undergrowth, the League joined other radicals in fighting his proposal. They were not only opposing Bush, but many responsible conservationists and experts who promote thinning and clearing underbrush as common sense prevention against forest fires.

The League has also become a leading advocate of permissive sex education in public schools, particularly in promoting "toleration" of the homosexual lifestyle.

It is funded by the Howard Heinz Endowment ($150,000 in 2002); Vira Heinz Endowment ($150,000 in 2002); William and Flora Hewitt Foundation ($150,000 in 2003); Summit Charitable Foundation ($150,000 in 2002); Pew Charitable Trusts; Turner Foundation ($570,000 from 2000-2002) and many others.

Incredibly, under President Bill Clinton, liberal appointees controlling the taxpayer-funded Environmental Protection Agency sabotaged their own administration by doling out $378,000 to the League. The League was attacking the EPA while that agency was funding it!

## League of Conservation Voters

The Sierra Club's David Brower— beloved by many super-rich foundations— pops up again, this time as the founder of the Washington-D.C.-based League of Conservation Voters. In 1969 he founded "a political voice for the national environmental movement." But the "voice" of Brower's Frankensteinian creation is far from the reasonable tone of a Teddy Roosevelt-style conservationist. The LCV lives on after Brower's death trumpeting a shrill Marxist-tinged, anti-business tone. It makes no bones that it is a member of the "Shadow Democratic Party," a nationwide group of nonprofits which campaign for left-wing Democrat candidates.

The LCV emulates the Christian Coalition by publishing and distributing political scorecards. It rates candidates on environmental stances and— surprise!— they show most Republicans scoring low and most Democrats high. Who assigns the grades? Activists from groups including the Environmental Working Group, the Sierra Club and Friends of the Earth (another Brower creation).

Scorers gave President Bush an "F" on the environment in 2003, setting the stage for an endorsement of Democrat John Kerry for president in 2004. Never mind that Kerry's wife is a major donor to the LCV through her Heinz foundations. This incestuous interlocking continues with the LCV's chairman Bill Roberts. He used to work for the Environmental Defense Fund, which was overseen by board member Teresa Heinz Kerry.

The California chapter signed onto the aforementioned 2003 document published by Environmentalists Against War citing "reasons" to oppose an attack on Iraq— all from an anti-American slant.

Aside from Heinz money, LCV receives major gifts from the Bullit Foundation, the Nathan Cummings Foundation, the William and Flora Hewlett Foundation, the Joyce Foundation, the David and Lucille Packard Foundation and the Turner Foundation.

## Natural Resources Defense Council

*The Bush administration is quietly putting radical new policies in place that will let its corporate allies poison our air, foul our water and devastate our wildlands for decades to come.*

That's the hysterical claim by Robert F. Kennedy Jr. in a recent fundraising letter on behalf of the New York City-based Natural Resources Defense Council.

The NRDC has a shameful record of attacking and shaking down corporate America and a gullible public. Its guru, the aforementioned David Fenton, flatly admits (as published in *The Wall Street Journal*), "We designed (the anti-Alar campaign) so that revenue would flow back to the NRDC from the public, and we sold a book about pesticides through a 900 number and the 'Donahue' show..."

What was the anti-Alar campaign? The preservative Alar was falsely identified in the late 1980s by Fenton and various other activists as being a cause of cancer. Half-baked scientific research was released to the news media which caused consumer panic about Alar in apples and resulted in an estimated loss of over $250 million for the apple industry. It was the Environmental Protection Agency which finally helped set the record straight, announcing that an individual would have to eat 50,000 pounds of Alar-tested apples per day over the course of a lifetime in order to digest enough to get cancer.

DiscovertheNetworks.org notes that Wendy Gordon Rockefeller was an NRDC staff member and research associate of Fenton's who helped initiate the scare. She was apparently enjoying herself so much that, along with actress Meryl Streep, she co-founded something called Mothers and Others for a Livable Planet. The new organization joined Fenton and others in fanning the Alar hoax. (Rockefeller serves as a director for Rockefeller Philanthropy Advisors and is vice president of the Rockefeller Family Fund. In recent years these foundations have given grants to environmental groups associated with the Mothers — including over $600,000 to Environmental Media Services, a Fenton-owned company primarily responsible for ruining the apple industry.)

Chief NRDC financiers are the Pew Charitable Trusts, which kicked in over $11 million between 1991 and 2002, and the Tides Foundation, which during the same period donated almost $500,000. According to its federal 990 tax form records, the group has become such a donor favorite that annual revenue jumped from around $36 million in 1999 to nearly $60 million in 2003. Having Hollywood actors Robert Redford and Pierce Brosnan as high-profile board members helps bring in more cash as well.

The NRDC partnered with the Sierra Club to run anti-Bush administration radio ads in 2004 and, the next year, endorsed a so-called "Earth Charter" that blames capitalism for the planet's environmental ills. The Charter says that,

> ... *the dominant patterns of production and*
> *consumption are causing environmental devastation,*

*the depletion of resources and a massive extinction of species. The benefits of development are not shared equitably and the gap between the rich and poor is widening.*

## Nature Conservancy

The Arlington, Va.-based Nature Conservancy appears to be the largest and wealthiest environmental pressure group, with 2004 general revenues totaling $732 million. Once a moderate force seeking to protect plants, animals and nature, it is one of many groups hijacked by extremists financed by the super-rich. Sierra Club founder David Brower admitted to the magazine *E* that he pushed his group to be more radical so that the radical Nature Conservancy would "look reasonable"— a devious strategy.

TNC often buys private lands, supposedly for conservation, but its concern for property owners' rights often goes out the window. In November 2004 it opposed, along with the Sierra Club, an Oregon ballot measure to provide compensation to owners whose property is devalued by regulations barring development— rules which are not surprisingly backed by the Conservancy. In an August 2005 *Boston Globe* interview, TNC President Stephen McCormick acknowledged that he believes big government is essential to his group's cause: "Regulation and buying land alone probably won't be sufficient for conservation to take hold on a really large scale,"

The group targets military bases in the name of "conservation." It pressures the U.S. military to establish "buffer zones" around bases surrounded by "critical wildlife habitats." It claims that encroaching development can create conflicts between training activities and local residents and says that "development reduces habitat for key species, increasing the burden on the Army land managers." Of course, as wryly pointed out by DiscovertheNetworks.org, the "burden" TNC refers to is one imposed by the group itself when it slams the military for attacking "habitat."

One of the Conservancy's main projects is the "Climate Change Initiative" and support for the Kyoto emissions protocol, which was unanimously rejected by the U.S. Senate. The TNC website is an encyclopedia of alarmist analysis. One claim is that "research shows the world has now become hotter than at any time during the past 1,000 years." Scientists of course differ, with many pointing out there have been cycles of cooling and warming and that the overall rise has only been mild, about six-tenths of one degree. And even that slight increase doesn't signal danger, as stories on the TNC website would indicate. Furthermore, the site refers to Hurricane Katrina in 2005 as evidence of "a growing number of severe weather events linked to global change"— another disputed claim among experts who monitor hurricane activity. In fact, the 2006 season logged the lowest number of hurricanes in years.

The Capital Research Center cites TNC as one of the top 10 nonprofit recipients of corporate contributions in 2002, with the group garnering approximately $1.5 million in corporate donations. However, in a series of 2003 investigative reports, *The Washington Post* exposed unethical fund-raising that took place in conjunction with its land purchases:

> *(T)he charity buys raw land, attaches some development restrictions and then resells the properties to supporters at greatly reduced prices. Buyers give the Conservancy cash payments for roughly the amount of the discount, a sum that is then written off the buyers' federal income taxes.*

In one of several cases detailed by the newspaper, TNC helped a trustee purchase a 146-acre Kentucky parcel for a horse farm and two houses. TNC acquired the property, valued at $368,000 under a conservation easement barring industrial development, and then shamelessly resold the land to the trustee for $252,000 (who then made up the remaining cost with a hefty charitable donation to the TNC). In response, the IRS conducted an audit of the organization in 2004 and issued a ruling which disallowed inappropriate tax deductible donations to charitable organizations in exchange for real estate.

The newspaper series further revealed TNC had extended a $1.55 million home loan to its president at a discounted interest rate—which it misreported. McCormick later hurried to repay the loan after the story's publication.

In June 2005 the U.S. Senate Finance Committee, after a two-year probe, issued a stinging report critical of the size of the tax breaks claimed by the Conservancy's supporters and private "side deals" with Conservancy "insiders." What was really embarrassing, though, was the *Post* discovery that the organization actually drilled for oil and natural gas on a Texas wildlife preserve where there was a breeding ground for an endangered species of grouse. TNC had been awarded the land from the Mobil oil company with the stipulation that it would protect the area. TNC quickly stopped its drilling, which it euphemistically called "resource extraction activities."

## Rainforest Action Network

"It is the savviest environmental agitator in the business," warns *The Wall Street Journal.* "We'll boycott a corporation until the end of the Earth if we have to," says Rainforest Action Network president Randall Hayes. That is no idle threat, since the San Francisco-based nonprofit's website lists an annual operating budget of over $3 million and 36 full-time workers dedicated to "non-violent direct action" spanning the globe.

The previous chapter on the Ford Foundation outlines RAN's virulent anti-capitalist bent— and why it is such a Ford favorite. RAN's history on its website is replete with how it smeared companies like Home Depot and Citigroup until they bowed to its "progressive" agenda. The website notes that it led a 1987 boycott of Burger King to protest the chain's use of beef from parts of the world where forests are cut to provide for cattle grazing. Burger King's sales dropped by 12 percent that year and RAN brags that the company finally stopped importing "rainforest beef."

Hayes has embarrassed mainstream liberals with his naked hatred of the Bush administration, especially by suggesting "the current administration may indeed have deliberately allowed 9/11 to happen, perhaps as a pretext to war." RAN endorsed the childish "10 Reasons Environmentalists Oppose the War in Iraq" document and went out on a limb by joining a 2002 Palestine Solidarity March which defended Palestinian suicide bombers.

This activity is approved by RAN's active and honorary board of directors which its website says include actor Woody Harrelson, singer Bonnie Raitt, actress Ali McGraw and musicians John Densmore and Bob Weir. RAN extremism is supported by annual gifts from Pew Charitable Trusts, the Blue Moon Fund and Rockefeller Brothers Fund.

## Sierra Club

The San Francisco-based Sierra Club, founded by famed conservationist John Muir, evolved in the 1960s from a group of nature enthusiasts into an influential organization of over 77,000 members with a $3 million-plus annual budget. The shift was accomplished by Berkeley, Ca., activist David Brower, the club's first executive director who died in 2000. His favorite phrase was, "All technology should be assumed guilty until proven innocent."

One measure of the extremism that grew within the group's ranks during the Brower years, and which was later fostered by executive director Carl Pope, was the 2003 election of Paul Watson to the board of directors. DiscovertheNetworks.org outlined his *modus operandi*:

> *Watson... oversees a small fleet of ships outfitted with cement-filled bows built for the sole purpose of violently ramming and sinking vessels he considers to be enemies of the environment— be they large whaling ships or small fishing boats. Each of Watson's boats is equipped with a high-powered water cannon and is protected by electrical barbed wire. Watson has also used acid, explosives and an AK-47 assault rifle to disable and sink 'enemy' ships. Far*

*from a departure from his normative tactics, Watson's maritime militancy was consistent with his declaration at a 2003 Animal Rights convention: 'There's nothing wrong with being a terrorist, as long as you win. Then you write the history.'*

Dick Lamm, former Democratic governor of Colorado, laments how just one wealthy donor influenced the Sierra Club's longtime stance on immigration control.

"Currently immigration policy, which many are trying to liberalize, will leave our grandkids an America of 1 billion Americans," he writes in *The Social Contract* (Fall 2006). "No matter argues The Sierra Club, overpopulation is only a global problem." Lamm, who ran unsuccessfully for the board as part of an immigration control slate, says David Gelbaum, a math wizard who made millions on Wall Street, contributed $101 million to the Sierra Club in 2004. "Gelbaum ... admitted that he had earlier warned the club 'if they ever came out anti-immigration they would never get a dollar from me.'" The real story, the former governor charges, "is that the Sierra Club's policy positions are for sale." He writes that the Club sold out when it came to confronting the issue of rising illegal and legal immigration— one of the truly important environmental issues of 21st century America.

The Sierra Club lost its tax exempt status years ago because of blatant political crusading (it endorsed John Kerry for president in 2004). Yet infighting over immigration, and the fact that gifts are no longer tax-exempt, hasn't diminished its attraction. It remains a popular repository for donors including the Rockefeller Brothers Fund, the Bullit Foundation, the William and Flora Hewitt Foundation, the Pew Charitable Trusts and the Turner Foundation.

## Union of Concerned Scientists

Students and faculty at the Massachusetts Institute of Technology formed the non-profit Union of Concerned Scientists in 1969 with a mission to build "a cleaner, healthier environment and a safer world." Since then its website notes the UCS has railed against everything from gas-guzzling SUVs to the imminent dangers of alleged global warming.

A petition with signatures from 1,600 scientists, collected by the UCS, demanded that the United States ratify the aforementioned Kyoto protocol that sought to eliminate carbon dioxide emissions in the West while exempting those emanating from Third World giants China and India. (Interestingly, after the petition was released, another — signed by 17,000 scientific experts— refuted the UCS's assertions about global warming.)

UCS president Kevin Knobloch repeatedly clashed with the Bush administration, accusing it of "politicizing science." Signers of a UCS declaration entitled "Restoring Scientific Integrity in Policy Making" beat their breasts as followers of "objective" science working for the common good. Yet DiscovertheNetworks.org found over half were "outed" as Democratic Party contributors. UCS "objectivity" took another hit in 2003 when congressional legislation, based on UCS-compiled research, was introduced aimed at banning the use of eight classes of antibiotics in livestock. After the debate began, the UCS conceded that many of its claims were speculative.

UCS propaganda on its website also touts the alleged dangers of genetically modified food— although many experts, including World Health Organization officials, affirm the safety of such food.

Donors include the Ford Foundation, the Carnegie Corp. of New York, the William and Flora Hewlett Foundation, the Joyce Foundation, the John D. and Catherine T. MacArthur Foundation, the David and Lucille Packard Foundation, the Blue Moon Fund, the Turner Foundation and the Pew Charitable Trusts.

## U. S. Public Interest Research Group

It was the early 1970s when PIRG chapters began flexing their muscle on campuses across the nation. Founded by Ralph Nader, the chapters kick in a percentage of funds raised— often from unsuspecting student governments who fund it with student fees— and send it to state and national bodies for lobbying and "educational" activities. The national office, of course, aggressively solicits foundation grants.

Although the primary focus is on the environment, U.S. PIRG executive director Gene Karpinski argued in favor of phony campaign finance reform legislation which later passed Congress as BICRA or the McCain-Feingold law. "The right to speak freely is our nation's highest value, but democracy also requires protecting alternative voices from being drowned out by a flood of cash," Karpinski said. He held that "unless we set limits on campaign spending, the powerful can continue to broadcast their voices, while the less powerful are barely heard." After the law passed in 2002— and after a heartbreakingly unsuccessful U.S. Supreme Court challenge— the exact opposite occurred. Lawyer Ken Starr, who this author worked with when president of the Atlanta-based Southeastern Legal Foundation, rightly warned at the time that issue advocacy ads mentioning the names of members of Congress would be heavily restricted.

In 2000 the group published *Storm Warning: Global Warming and the Rising Cost of Extreme Weather*, which predictably blamed automobiles and power plants for the rise of temperatures. It also joined other environmental groups pushing for implementation of the Kyoto Protocol. It continues an anti-nuclear power crusade and its website in early 2007 trumpeted that Maryland PIRG was fighting a proposed new nuclear reactor.

DiscovertheNetworks.org has found that the Seattle-based Wilburforce Foundation is a major PIRG donor, funneling $120,000 in grants to just the PIRG Education Fund's Arctic Wilderness Campaign between 2001 and 2004. The website notes: "Nathan Manuel, who has directed U.S. PIRG's Arctic Wilderness Campaign since 1998, remains one of the leading foes of Alaskan drilling, exhorting other environmentalist groups to pressure the U.S. Senate to vote against its allowance." The Bauman Family Foundation is another PIRG sugar daddy. Headed by activist Patricia Bauman, it doled out $1,475,000 in grants between 1996 and 2002.

# Waterkeeper Alliance

This Tarrytown, N.Y.-based alliance of 120 activist groups, founded in 1999 by Robert F. Kennedy Jr., ought to be called the Waterkeeper and Lawyers Friendship Society. According to Activistcash.com, since his 1984 conviction for heroin possession Kennedy first worked for the Natural Resources Defense Council and then assumed a Pace University law professorship specifically to sue governments and businesses on behalf of the Riverkeeper organization.

DiscovertheNetworks.org found that the Alliance filed trademark claims on words such as "waterkeeper," "lakekeeper," "baykeeper" and "coastkeeper," and requires environmental groups seeking to use such names to license with the Alliance in order to do so. "Kennedy says this is to ensure the integrity of this 'brand' name and prevent its misuse by capitalists, but critics see it as his way of exerting control and influence over both new and preexisting environmental groups— and of making money from any commercial use of these long-used 'keeper' names," the website notes.

Kennedy enjoys sticking it to "right-wingers" and "capitalists." How extreme Kennedy really is was underscored when this author witnessed him loudly applauding during a 2000 Hollywood fund-raiser when a speaker noted that actor Christopher Reeve's father was "a proud Communist." Most of the liberals in attendance didn't go that far.

The self-proclaimed Waterkeeper "president" loves to sue, is always in search of a sympathetic judge or jury and has a coterie of law firms that cut so many corners it would embarrass the writers of ABC-TV's "Boston Legal" show. When assembling his legal team in 2000, each firm had to ante up $50,000 apiece in order to work with him to sue businesses in the U.S. and foreign countries, especially the pork industry.

After continued attempts using federal racketeering (RICO) statutes against pork producers in seeking huge damage awards, federal judge Elizabeth Kovachevich declared: "After detailing the reasons why plaintiffs did not have a claim under RICO … plaintiffs again brought a RICO claim, against this court's advice." Kennedy's lawsuit, she wrote, "failed to state anything at all, except conclusory allegations that have no support." Such recklessness surfaced again in July 2003 when a major U.S. pork producer secured an indictment in Poland against the Waterkeeper Alliance for committing slander during an inflammatory rant against the company's Polish subsidiary. It charged Kennedy and his lawyers disseminated "untrue information" and "consciously manipulated the facts."

ActivistCash.com points to Kennedy's harshest public thrashing from, of all people, Riverkeeper founder Robert Boyle and seven others on that group's board. They angrily resigned in 2000 after Kennedy insisted upon hiring a convicted environmental felon, William Wegner, as the group's chief scientist. At the time, Boyle told the *New York Post* that Kennedy "is very reckless," adding "(h)e's assumed an arrogance above his intellectual stature." In a *New York Times* interview, Boyle slammed harder: "(h)e was thinking of himself and not the cause of the river. It all became his own greater glory."

Prime funding for the Waterkeepers comes from Kennedy's trial lawyers and from the Vira I. Heinz Endowment.


## Wilderness Society

The website of this Washington, D.C.-based non-profit, founded in 1935, makes a good pitch: "Some of America's natural lands are just too wild to drill. But if the government has its way, some 118,000 leases will be let, sacrificing some of our most spectacular landscapes to oil and gas development," its website proclaims. This author, however, could never verify the 118,000 number with government sources.

Its website slams oil exploration in the small 2,000-acre section of the 19.5-million acre Arctic National Wildlife Refuge (ANWR) in Alaska. Yet opening ANWR would help break future dependence on foreign oil while not harming the environment. The U.S. Energy

Department estimates ANWR could yield more than 800 million barrels of oil annually, calling it the largest "unexplored, potentially productive offshore basin in the United States."

Society head William Meadows spouts typical Democratic Party talking points, such as the Bush administration "has declared war on the environment"— rhetoric designed to boost fund-raising. DiscovertheNetworks.org ironically notes Meadows ignored President Bill Clinton's 1995 "salvage logging rider" initiative which doubled the amount of logging in U.S. forests by exempting the logging industry from environmental regulations. That was a glaring omission — a favor to a liberal president— since the Society has long sought to ban logging from America's forests.

The Society approves of thinning excessive forest undergrowth through controlled fires, but its website indicates it opposes logging enterprises that accomplish the same goal. Why? In its warped world, fire is acceptable because there's no financial reward to humans. If George W. Bush (but not Clinton) supports timber-cutting to thin dense undergrowth and deadwood in forests, then that is "profit-driven" intervention by capitalists. Most experts agree, however, that judicious, systematic tree clearing lowers the odds that runaway fires could destroy large woodland tracts. The U.S. General Accounting Office reported several years ago: "The most extensive and serious problem (facing) national forests in the interior West is the over-accumulation of vegetation... 39 million acres are at risk."

Michael Betsch of the Cybercast News Service found the Society is sloppy regarding scientific information it distributes to schools. He reported that when it wanted to introduce students to Earth Day and the Wilderness Movement, the curriculum for schoolteachers (k through 12) was developed by a volunteer who— as the Society's manager of electronic communications Kathy Kilmer admitted— had "no formal science background." Jeff Stier of the American Council of Science and Health, says:

*Environmental dogma has invaded the classroom. What's so troubling is that it starts popping up in textbooks and it appears in the curriculum, especially at the elementary school levels ... Promoting an environmental agenda does not promote science education. Rather, it promotes a political agenda which is not an appropriate forum ... Whenever you have activist groups appealing to educators to promote an agenda, there should be cause for concern.*

Disseminating propaganda to public schools is primarily why Pew Charitable Trusts donated over $3 million since 1996 for "educational" purposes. Other donors include the Bullit Foundation, the David and Lucille Packard Foundation, the Nathan Cummings Foundation, the Rockefeller Brothers Fund, the William and Flora Hewlett Foundation and the Turner Foundation.

## Wildlands Conservancy

This organization, founded in 1995 and based in Oak Glen, Va., essentially acts as the intermediary between property owners and the federal government when it purchases property that it later "donates" to the federal government.

In one of the largest sales of private land in American history, DiscovertheNetworks.org found the Conservancy in 1999 negotiated with the U.S. Bureau of Land Management to buy 640,000 acres in the Mohave Desert from the Catellus Development Corp. The land was then donated back to the bureau to create a national preserve. *CounterPunch* reported that a left-wing political friend of the Conservancy also benefited. U.S. Sen. Diane Feinstein, D-Ca., who crafted the Desert Wildlands Act that enables such land deals, received over $150,000 in campaign donations from Catellus.

These shenanigans prompted the liberal *Los Angeles Times* to disdainfully editorialize that the Conservancy has been "swapping real estate with the gusto of a 19th century land baron," ostensibly to prevent development.

The September 20, 2002 issue of *Forbes* also notes how environmentalists like the Conservancy have come up with "an ingenious way" to acquire land: "Just confiscate it." It chronicles this scenario: The Environmental Protection Agency creates a *de facto* wildlife sanctuary on private land by saying that the ducks on it must not be disturbed. If the land coveted by the government is dry "a different statute is cited and different birds (spotted owls) are sent in as an occupation force. The effect, in either case, is to increase the public's land holdings. For free," The magazine rightly condemns such land-use control as worthy of a dictatorship.

Co-founder David Gelbaum (the open borders advocate who also donates heavily to the Sierra Club and a variety of Democratic candidates), has given the Conservancy "at least $250 million" according to the Los *Angeles Times.* According to TWC records, the respective values of the land it has donated to the federal government totaled $2.7 million in 2003, $2.3 million in 2002 and $7.9 million in 2001.

## World Resources Institute

The website of this notorious Washington, D.C.-based tax-exempt think tank lists assets totaling $5 million, annual revenue of over $20 million and boasts "a staff of 150 professionals from more than 20 nations, connected to a network of advisors, collaborators, international fellows and partner institutions in more than 50 countries." It attacks free enterprise, promotes adoption of the Kyoto pact and believes the United States should transfer environmental decision-making to the United Nations. WRI also conducts a "Beyond Grey Pinstripes" class program in which business school students and young professionals working within the private enterprise system are indoctrinated into a utopian, socialist mindset supposedly devoid of corporate scandal.

Established in 1982, $15 million in start-up money came from the John D. and Catherine T. MacArthur Foundation, plus $10 million more from the Rockefeller and Andrew K. Mellon foundations. Founders include George Woodall, who helped establish the aforementioned Natural Resources Defense Council; Murray Hellmann, a Clinton disciple who's a former MacArthur Foundation director; and James Speth, who heads the United Nations Development Program.

Jonathan Lash, a former Natural Resources Defense Council lawyer who now heads WRI, is a constant Bush administration critic regarding Kyoto and global warming.      Former Clinton Agriculture Secretary Dan Glickman is a prominent WRI board member as is William Ruckleshaus, a liberal Republican who headed the federal Environmental Protection Agency (EPA) under President Richard Nixon. (Ruckelshaus was responsible for the 1972 ban of the pesticide DDT.)

Perhaps most galling is that this tax-exempt outfit received taxpayer money from the EPA. For over a decade— mainly during the Clinton administration— its records indicate the institute received an average of $2.7 million in annual government funding, with an all-time high topping $5 million in 1998. The Competitive Enterprise Institute also found WRI used EPA "global warming grants" to help promote U.S. Senate passage of the ill-fated Kyoto pact that was later unanimously rejected by the U.S. Senate.

The usual suspects fund this think tank: the Ford Foundation, the MacArthur Foundation, the Nathan Cummings Foundation, the Pew Charitable Trusts, the William and Flora Hewlett Foundation, the David and Lucille Packard Foundation, the W.K. Kellogg Foundation and the Rockefeller and Turner foundations. The Bill and Melinda Gates Foundation and the AT&T Foundation have also been roped in for grants.

# FOUNDATIONS TARGET EVANGELICALS
## CHAPTER VI

*"Breathing, building a fire to cook or keep warm, driving a car or tractor, or burning oil to produce electricity ... (are) morally good and necessary activities that God intended for us. It seems very unlikely to me that God would have set up the earth to work in such a way that these good and necessary activities would actually destroy the earth." – Wayne Grudem, Phoenix Seminary research professor.*

What a surprise in December 2006 when the Atlanta-based Weather Channel announced its "First One Degree Hot List" of those people "most influential in global climate change." One of the winners picked by the politically correct channel, besides former Vice President Al Gore, was the National Association of Evangelicals and its vice president for governmental affairs, the Rev. Richard Cizik. They were cited for their "enviro-religious concept known as creation care."

National Association of Evangelicals? Creation care? What's all this about?

Welcome a new player, funded and prodded by leftist foundations. It is yet another religious organization promoting a "creation care" ethic and an "Evangelical Climate Initiative" that assists foundations promoting one-world government, abortion on demand and even pagan ideologies. Since the National Association of Evangelicals has been placed in an adversarial position on this issue to that of conservative Christian groups and churches that have heretofore been its allies, the secular left could not be happier.

Sad to say, many sincere evangelicals aren't looking at the bigger picture.

Funding the Association, which claims to represent hundreds of denominations, is a clever attempt to give the anti-Christian agenda of leftist foundations and their allies the moral cover before the public that they've never before enjoyed. "Our fear is that evangelical leaders who in good faith associated themselves with the ECI are being exploited by organizations that not only deny their biblically-based value system, but hold such beliefs in contempt," says Dr. Jay Richards, a research fellow at the Acton Institute for the Study of Religion and Liberty.

The ECI was launched in February 2006 with 86 prominent supporters arguing "this is God's world and any damage that we do to God's world is an offense against God Himself." ECI proponents at that time, while calling for federal legislation to reduce carbon dioxide emissions, wildly predicted that "millions of people could die in this century" because "most of the climate change problem is human induced."

Among prominent evangelicals who signed off on the ECI are author and pastor Rick Warren, *Christianity Today* editor David Neff, Pastor Jack Heyford and former National Association of Evangelicals vice president for governmental affairs Robert P. Dugan.

Remember the William and Flora Hewlett Foundation? It donated $475,000 to specifically launch the ECI "Christian Climate Change" advertising campaign. (It would surprise most Christians if they knew that this "charity" religiously funds abortion-on-demand groups.)

Consider just one deceptive Hewlett-funded TV ad that aired in 2006. It begins with a voice— accompanied by a soothing picture of a traditional church replete with steeple— intoning, "Did you know that evangelical leaders are telling us that global warming must be stopped? Because it will bring more devastating floods, droughts and disease." (Then there's a shot of a poor black child looking wistfully into the camera.) The ad continues: "As Christians, our faith in Jesus Christ compels us to love our neighbors and to be good stewards of God's creation. The good news is that with God's help we can stop global warming for our kids, our world and our Lord." (The text and website address then pops up on the screen: The Evangelical Climate Initiative— Join Our Call to Action. www.ChristianandClimate.org.)

The slick-talking Elmer Gantry could not have made a better pitch. Nor could the money-loving, circuit-riding preacher played by Steve Martin in "Leap of Faith."

## Latter-day false prophets

Great lions of modern Christianity like the Rev. Billy Graham, Bishop Fulton Sheen and C.S. Lewis converted millions to their faith while teaching and comforting the faithful. These Paladins of God were Bible-based enemies of the collectivism known as big government— the device which reduces the many mansions of God's universe to a stockyard feeding the greed of hidden forces. The work of those eloquent apostles is being undercut by wolves in clerical garb who take their 30 pieces of silver from foundations and their shills to pedal "ecology theology" and the latest "climate change" propaganda line.

James Spann, the courageous television meteorologist quoted in the first chapter, effectively rebuts the new hucksters:

> *The climate of this planet has been changing ever since God put the planet here. It will always change, and the warming in the past 10 years is not much different than the warming we saw in the 1930s and other decades. And, let's not forget we are at the*

*end of the ice age in which ice covered most of North America and Northern Europe.*

*If you don't like to listen to me, find another meteorologist with no tie to grant money for research on the subject. I would not listen to anyone who is a politician, a journalist or someone in science who is generating money from this issue.*

Spann should also have cautioned against listening to leaders of the National Association of Evangelicals and National Council of Churches.

The New York City-based NCC, an umbrella group of Protestant and Orthodox denominations, has become a lapdog seduced by money from left-wing foundations including those controlled by atheists George Soros and Ted Turner. For decades the church council has been losing members (and contributions) to traditional houses of worship because of its "social gospel" activities like lobbying Congress against voluntary school prayer, for big-spending welfare programs and, during the Cold War, advocating unilateral disarmament by the United States. At the international level, the NCC provided monetary support to its world council for violent black guerrilla groups in Africa.

In 2006 the influential Institute on Religion and Democracy released a white paper "Strange Yokefellows: The National Council of Churches and its Growing Non-Church Constituency." It found that with dues from member churches dropping the NCC made up the difference with gifts from the Ford Foundation, the Tides Foundation, the Rockefeller Brothers Fund, Turner's United Nations Foundation, Soros' Open Society Institute, the Carnegie Corporation of New York, the Robert Wood Johnson Foundation, the National Religious Partnership for the Environment, the John L. and James S. Knight Foundation, the Sierra Club, the American Association of Retired Persons and even left-wing actress Vanessa Redgrave among others. These grants go to projects ranging from support for the Kyoto pact and the United Nations (Soros and Turner interests) to "ecojustice work" and "interfaith dialogue."

118

The NCC even received $25,000 in 2004-2005 for a political advocacy "peace" project from the Massachusetts-based Columbe Foundation, whose parent Proteus Fund donates to groups supporting homosexual rights and same-sex marriage.

At the end of fiscal year 2005, the Institute on Religion and Democracy reported the NCC took $1.76 million from secular foundations and non-church groups.

Ralph Reed, executive director of the Christian Coalition from 1989 to 1997, knows most of today's NCC and evangelical players. He tells this author:

> *Evangelicals take seriously the Biblical call to be good stewards of God's creation. But any attempt to equate that legitimate principle with the policies advocated by the radical environmental movement— the Kyoto treaty, mandatory caps on carbon emissions, and job-killing taxes and regulation— will not resonate at the grassroots of America among people of faith. The jury is still out on the science of climate change.*

Indeed, as reported by the March 3, 2007 *New York Times,* the leaders of several traditional Christian groups in a letter to the National Association of Evangelicals said "we have observed that Cizik and others are using the global warming controversy to shift the emphasis away from the great moral issues of our time." They concluded that if Cizik, a longtime Washington lobbyist, "cannot be entrusted to articulate the views of American evangelicals," then he should be encouraged to resign. (Cizik, as reported in that same *Times* article, claims that he experienced a profound "conversion" on the climate warming issue in 2002 after attending a retreat.)

## In the beginning, ecology

The genesis of the effort to convince American churches to promote unscientific environmental policies began in the early 1970s at New York City's Cathedral of St. John the Divine. The nation's largest liberal Episcopal Church was already abandoning the holy Bible for the Gospel of St. Trendy, typified by its blasphemous display of a life-size female crucifix dubbed "Christa." In the words of writer Mick Kronman, the church became the first "mecca for Mother Earth worshipers who believe animals, plants and even rocks have spirits and human-level rights." The cutting-edge "New Age" church and its disciples around the country began preaching a simplistic philosophy that "crimes against the earth" are a sin and "creation care" is the new salvation.

The major left-wing foundations and their allies, including the United Nations, quickly took notice of this trend.

In the meantime, the Cathedral of St. John the Divine became headquarters to an outfit called the Temple of Understanding. The Temple is an official UN non-government "observer," making it a partner in the world organization's agenda. A key Temple promoter— who served as secretary-general of the UN Earth Summit— is Maurice Strong who once declared: "Isn't the only hope for the planet that the industrialized civilizations collapse? Isn't it our responsibility to bring that about?"

One of the Temple's directors is the Rev. Thomas Berry, who actually tells readers of his book *Dream of the Earth* (published by Sierra Club Books) that "we should place less emphasis on Christ as a person and a redeemer."

Strong and Berry have worked closely with St. John Pastor James Morton, who calls his church a "Green Cathedral." Morton also states:

> *Religion binds the whole cosmos starting from above, ecology binds the whole cosmos starting from below. Together they are the heaven and earth of the understanding that we urgently need in the new millennium.*

Further underscoring how wacky "sacred ecology" theology has become, St. John's offers prayers for endangered species— even algae. St. John's clergy mock the traditional Biblical view of Creation as a resource over which God's human children were given dominion and in which human life possesses intrinsic value. The new evangelicals want to somehow secure the well-being of every animal and organism, including algae.

Alan Cooperman in a Jan. 12, 2007 *Washington Post* piece writes,

> *Environmental activists are even coaxing uninformed churches into the belief that abstention (from meat and fish) and charity for the fish in 'God's Blue Acre' are means of salvation and ascension into heaven. Even Christ's crucifixion has been linked to the suffering of animals and spoiling of an otherwise pure earth, to convince and convert church laity.* (By the way, Jesus ate fish and also the Passover meal that included lamb.)

In *Ecology as Religion, Faith In Place of Fact,* Cato Institute essayist Doug Bandow warns that this kind of environmentalism turns Christian stewardship into a sacred ritual. In essence, it's nothing more than a pagan religion in which Earth replaces God as the focus of worship.

"A recent issue of a magazine from one of Minnesota's Lutheran colleges features a picture of the campus pastor, wearing a beanie with a propeller on it. He is leading what the magazine calls a 'congregation' of students in a dedication 'service' at the foot of a giant new wind turbine that provides power to the campus," writes Katherine Kersten in the Feb. 7, 2007 Minneapolis-St. Paul *Star Tribune.* "At one point the pastor asked the students to raise their own miniature pinwheels. I could almost imagine them all being suddenly borne aloft by a gust of prairie wind during the closing verse of a great old Lutheran hymn." Kersten went on to report that Catholic and Lutheran leaders joined polar explorer Will Steger to lobby the

Minnesota legislature on what the religious leaders called the moral imperative of addressing climate change.

Unfortunately, since 1993, more evangelical converts have been singing from the foundation-funded "eco-justice" hymnal. That was the year the Ford and Rockefeller foundations, the Pew Charitable Trusts, the Nathan Cummings Foundation, the Turner, Syrdna and C.S. Mott foundations, the New World Foundation and others donated over $5 million to ensure that America's Christians and Jews would place environmental issues at the heart of their religious life.

The foundations' vehicle to conduct the ambitious campaign— directed at 67,000 congregations consisting of more than 100 million churchgoers— was to be the National Religious Partnership for the Environment. The Oct. 5 1993 kickoff rally occurred at the Mount Gilead Baptist Church in Washington, D.C. The mission: "To underscore the connection between addressing issues of poverty and the environment."

The "partnership" launched that day was actually a formal plan of action between four of the major environmentalist cheerleaders of the day— the NCC, the U.S. Catholic Conference, the Coalition on the Environment and Jewish Life and the Evangelical Environment Network. The NCC general secretary, the Rev. Joan Brown Campbell, stressed the overall goal would be to make global warming "a litmus test for the faith community." Clergy allied with the cause soon thereafter began preaching about "eco-justice"— promoting only those economic policies "in harmony" with mother Earth.

The Partnership operated in its early years out of— where else? — the Cathedral of St. John the Divine. There's no doubt its campaign has been making inroads, fostered by thousands of copies of slick educational "action kits," sermons and Sunday School material prepared for every faith and denomination. Religious leaders of all stripes are regularly recruited into Partnership training seminars, where they are re-educated with new clichés and dogmas.

Since 1993, other left-wing foundations have joined in backing the Partnership, including the Blue Moon Fund and the MacArthur

Foundation. Hewlett, the sugar daddy of the National Association of Evangelicals, periodically kicks in to the collection plate. It bestowed $400,000 in June 2005 alone. The Turner Foundation donated almost $1 million to the Partnership from 1993-2002.

## Evangelical eco lobbying

Writer and property rights activist Joanna Waugh says that "at the community level, most churches believe the Partnership is about recycling, energy and weather conservation, and creating wildlife habitat on church property." Waugh also recalls that evangelical churchgoers began lobbying their members of Congress on environmental issues after the Republican takeover in the 1994 election. She writes of one example:

> *An August 1995 legislative action alert from the Evangelical Lutheran Church in North America urged its congregants to write their U.S. senators and 'assure them that their constituents want to maintain or increase— but certainly not reduce— protection of our wetlands ...' A sample letter to the editor was included in the action alert which read, '(The Wetlands Regulatory Reform Act of 1995) only benefits large businesses, oil and gas developers and real estate tycoons, while the neighbors of developers and agribusiness will suffer with flooded property and contaminated drinking water supplies...'*

Another example provided by Waugh is when the liberal church cabal went to war against the newly-elected Republican Congress which was bent on cutting the Environmental Protection Agency bureaucracy and its myriad regulations, as well as rewriting and reforming the Endangered Species Act.

The National Religious Partnership for the Environment submitted written testimony in 1995 opposing H.R. 2275, The Endangered Species Conservation and Management Act, by U.S. Reps. Don Young, R-Al, and Richard Pombo, R-Ca. The bill would have improved the scientific basis for listing and managing endangered species, provided voluntary incentives for private property owners to protect listed species on their land, established a Species Conservation Fund to carry out the Act and sought to include the states in endangered species conservation planning. It was complicated, but balanced, legislation, Yet Waugh noted that the Methodist Church in particular, "responded in a way that typifies the attitude of the Partnership members." "An analysis of (this) bill," the sanctimonious Methodists wrote, "clearly reveals that the primary motive behind this legislation is not to protect God's creation. We believe that the driving force behind this legislation is greed."

Such sanctimony was further evidenced in November 1995 when Clinton administration Interior Secretary Bruce Babbit gave an address before the Partnership. Consider part of his text, cleverly weaving in liberal environmental themes while sticking a knife into traditional Christianity:

> *(As) a child growing up in a small town in northern Arizona, I learned my religious values through the Catholic Church... (I)n that era, in that Judeo-Christian tradition, (the church) kept silent on our moral obligation to nature. In all the years I attended Sunday mass, hearing hundreds of homilies and sermons, there was never any reference, any link, to our natural heritage or to the spiritual meaning of the land surrounding us.*

> *Yet outside that church, I always had a nagging instinct that the vast landscape was somehow sacred, and holy, and connected to me in a sense that my catechism ignored. (Through a Hopi Indian friend), I came to believe, deeply and irrevocably, that the land... and all the plants and animals in the natural world are...a direct reflection of divinity... I understand why some members of Congress react with such unrestrained fear and loathing towards the Endangered Species Act. For if they heard that command from our Creator, if they truly listened to His instruction to be*

*responsible stewards, then their entire framework of human rationalizations for tearing apart the Act comes to naught.*

"What is special about this speech," syndicated columnist Alston Chase wrote, is the emphasis "that... environmentalism is a religious movement." No wonder the "eco-justice" crowd was so upset when their hero Al Gore didn't succeed Bill Clinton as president, and why they've displayed such un-Christlike hatred toward George W. Bush personally. They lost Babbit. The Interior Department, after he left in 2001, began undertaking more common-sense, scientific and balanced policies.

One other point: When conservative and mainstream Christian groups lobby secular lawmakers, or when Republicans propose giving tax money to faith-based organizations, liberals invariable trot out their "keep the separation of church and state" argument. Not so, of course, in this instance.

## Grantmakers in the temple

The political setback of the 2000 Bush election made leftist foundations work harder on their environmental/evangelical agenda, prompting the dispensing of more millions to their acolytes. "Information about church contributions are protected by federal law, but foundations like Rockefeller, W. Alton Jones and Pew Charitable Trusts underwrite biggies like the National Religious Partnership for the Environment," underscores Mike Barkey, an analyst for a Detroit-based Christian think tank.

Additional millions for eco-religious groups are provided by the Environmental Grantmakers Association. Described by the website Undueinfuence.com as an "incorporated networking organization for left-wing/anti-corporate environmental causes," it operates out of Rockefeller Brothers Fund offices, is controlled by Rockefeller employee Susan Hansen and accepts grants under the Rockefeller tax-exemption. It represents over 130 donor organizations, including companies like Waste Management, Chevron and foundations like

Ford and the Pew Charitable Trusts. The EGA does not give grants, its own website explains, but is a voluntary association of foundations and giving programs that hold strategy meetings to target funding. Among topics at its planning seminars have been schemes to derail the property rights movement as "anti-environmental" and, lately, ways to keep building a coalition with churches and how houses of worship can best be subjected to eco-indoctrination.

"Innocent people of faith are being preyed upon," warns Ron Arnold of the Center for Defense of Free Enterprise. "They don't understand complex environmental issues, yet they are encouraged to be 'Noah' congregations, where the Ark is equated to the Endangered Species Act. Changing the act, then, is considered sinking the ark. And that, of course, is a sin."

In January 2007, the National Association of Evangelicals and the Center for Health and Global Environment at Harvard University were at it again. Saying they shared a moral purpose, they trundled out an "Urgent Call to Action"— an alert about the dangers of the burning of fossil fuels and the extinction of species. They also announced development of a public relations tool called the "Creation Care" Bible study group. (It's instructive to note that Eric Chivian, director of the Harvard Center— which its website touts as an "official United Nations Environmental Programme collaborative center"— is a proponent of the Kyoto pact that would create a billion-dollar UN bureaucracy to redistribute wealth from the U.S. to the Third World through an elaborate carbon dioxide emissions trading system.)

Mainstream Christian leaders and groups are fighting back, however. The Interfaith Stewardship Alliance, a group of over 130 theologians, scientists and policy analysts, derided the "Urgent Call to Action" as "just another attempt to create the impression of growing consensus among evangelicals about global warming. There is no such growing consensus." The Alliance charged that the NAE board never approved the collaboration with Harvard (with the NAE board countering that it approved a "dialogue" but no specific action).

A point-by-point critique of the "Urgent Call to Action" from the Alliance argues:

*Claims of dangerous or catastrophic global warming are...based on grossly unrealistic assumptions about future energy use, dominant energy types, pollution levels, economic development and other factors that do not reflect current facts or unlikely future situations.*

The founder of the Alliance, Calvin Beisner of Knox Theological Seminary, said evangelicals should focus on helping the poor create wealth and on providing them with clean drinking water and medical care. Activities that produce carbon dioxide like "breathing, building a fire to cook or keep warm, driving a car or tractor or burning coal to produce electricity ... (are) morally good and necessary activities that God intended for us," says Alliance member and Phoenix Seminary Bible professor Wayne Grudem. "It seems very unlikely to me that God would have set up the earth to work in such a way that these good and necessary activities would actually destroy the earth."

Prominent leaders ranging from the Prison Ministries' Chuck Colson to Focus on the Family President Dr. James Dobson have criticized the NAE initiatives, calling them a "distraction" from the main missions of Christianity. Dr. Richard Land of the Southern Baptist Convention notes, "Among American evangelicals there is no consensus about the causes of global warming, or the solutions to global warming." They and others have asked evangelicals like megachurch pastor Joel Osteen and author/preacher Warren to back off the environmentalist binge— and Warren has to some extent. The board of the Christian Coalition in late 2006 even dumped its president-elect— the Rev. Joel Hunter of Northland Church in Longwood, Florida— for warming to the NAE and seeking to institute a climate change agenda.

Nevertheless, the money changers— or shall we say grantmakers— are in God's temple. Shame on Christians who do not take the whip to them and kick over their money-laden tables.

# SEXUAL MORALITY & THE FOUNDATIONS
## CHAPTER VII

*"Everything that was nailed down is done comin'*
*loose!" – The late U.S. Sen. Sam Ervin, D-N.C.*

Interest in human sexual behavior has been around since, well, Adam and Eve. Yet America's current wave of permissive sexuality didn't start with the 1969 Woodstock rock festival and its media-promoted "if it feels good, do it" philosophy. A workable plan to eventually dynamite America's Judeo-Christian sexual and marital mores was actually launched in the 1940s by amoral foundation elites and a willing tool, a frail zoologist from Hoboken, New Jersey named Alfred C. Kinsey.

Kinsey is often described in the mainstream media as "the father of America's sexual revolution." Columnist and one-time presidential candidate Patrick Buchanan accurately calls him "America's original dirty old man." Kinsey's career is the story of his unflagging promotion by the Rockefeller Foundation. It is also about the transformation of America.

Influencing Americans to accept sexual permissiveness and criminal behavior— including child sex— was a revolutionary concept when the president of the University of Indiana established the Kinsey Institute. Yet this permissiveness— Kinsey maintained, sexually speaking, there is no such thing as "normal" or "abnormal"— has taken root in the popular culture. Indeed, for the last 50 years, the sexual revolution spawned by his "research" has been a juggernaut which social and religious conservatives has sometimes been able to impede but which, thus far, they have definitely been unable to stop.

Kinsey's highly-publicized "scientific" work, ending with his 1956 death, bestowed to the left an unprecedented rationale for implementing wide legal and societal change. As the folksy Senator Ervin once complained from the Senate floor, "everything that was nailed down is comin' loose"— and even cursory research reveals Kinsey and the Rockefeller money behind him engineered how everything *did* come loose.

California State Sen. Raymond Haynes, in a July 25, 2000 letter to fellow legislators across the nation, framed the many implications of the media-ballyhooed 1948 release of Kinsey's *Sexual Behavior in the Human Male:*

> *State governments across our country continue to spend the taxpayers' money for programs and agencies based on Kinsey's skewed findings or that disseminate Kinseyism. Any accredited "sexuality"-related program, by definition, teaches Kinsey's pathological sexual license— and that results in out-of-wedlock births, venereal diseases and sexual and marriage dysfunction.*

## The genesis of the scheme

Studies on sex, sexual hormones and reproduction were well underway in America during the 1930s when Kinsey began receiving notice and backing for sex research. In an introduction to his *Male* volume, Kinsey explained where his funding originated:

*The present volume is a progress report from a case history study on human sex behavior. The study has been underway during the past nine years. Throughout these years it has had the sponsorship and support of Indiana University, and during the past six years the support of the National Research Council's Committee for Research on Problems of Sex, with funds granted by the Medical Division of the Rockefeller Foundation.*

Former Kinsey Institute advisor James H. Jones wrote an explosive bombshell of a biography in which he revealed Kinsey to be a sadomasochist and homosexual. He indicated that most of the "research" team shared the same proclivities. Dr. Judith Reisman, writing in the definitive *Kinsey: Crime & Consequences (Second Edition)*, documents that the Kinsey team's research for *Sexual Behavior in the Human Male* was far from an objective scientific quest for human betterment:

*Kinsey's aggressive, intrusive and arguably illegal conduct was protected by Indiana University's public relations apparatus. We now know that some of the women and children in publicity photographs may have paid a high price to maintain the carefully honed Kinsey image.*

In an October 1997 column, Mona Charen noted that "according to one wife of another employee, there was 'sickening pressure' to agree to have sex on film." Other outrageous examples of Kinsey's coercion and sexual blackmail, provided by biographer Jones and others in recent years, had the beneficial effect of finally knocking Kinsey off his once-esteemed liberal pedestal. Reisman writes:

*The only known 'straight' member of Kinsey's team, Vincent Nowlis, was hired due to his friendship with Robert Yerkes, Kinsey's Rockefeller Foundation mentor... During an interview with Yorkshire TV, he confirmed that his departure was the result of Kinsey's efforts to recruit him into the 'homosexual experience.' And, in the 1998 Yorkshire documentary, Kinsey's Paedophiles, (James) Jones recalls that 'Kinsey and other (male) members of the Institute staff show(ed) up in Vincent Nowlis' room, inviting him to disrobe with the clear understanding that sexual activity would follow.' Nowlis resigned quietly. Until the Jones interview, he never revealed the tainted research team, or the child sex abuse underpinning Kinsey's chapters on child sexuality.*

Especially revolting is how Kinsey categorized sundry sexual activities involving young children as sex "play," including abuse by adults. By reclassifying all sexual abuse of children as "play," Reisman notes, Kinsey logically reported no data on child rape and other forms of abuse.

Some inside the Rockefeller Foundation responsible for oversight of the grant actually complained about bad data and irregularities concerning research regarding the experiences of prisoners, bar-hopping homosexuals and child molesters. They noted there was never a trained mathematical statistician on the team. Warren Weaver, head of the foundation's natural sciences division, objected to funding Kinsey's "library of erotic literature, and a collection of pictures and other 'art' objects." Specifically, Weaver wrote:

> *... I remind you that I opposed this grant when it was discussed in officers' conference. Now this library-art aspect of their work surely requires, out of his total general budget ... more than the total annual amount the RF is contributing. I contend that it is perfectly realistic to say the RF is paying for this collection of erotica and for the activities directly associated with it. And I say further that I don't think we need to, or ought to.*

Rockefeller trustees obviously ordered the internal critics to ignore the distorted data. The ultimate foundation objective— to rewrite American law and ultimately to soften penalties for sex crimes — required that grants for publicity and publication would continue. Reisman writes:

> *With connections to the mass media via the Rockefeller organization, Kinsey was able to generate widespread public curiosity and interest in his book prior to publication. And selection of the prestigious medical publisher W.B. Saunders served to further enhance the impression that the book was an authentic scientific endeavor.*

Dr. Albert Hobbs of the University of Pennsylvania was an outspoken critic of Kinsey and his methods. He pointed to, among other flaws, the Institute's refusal to release all the basic data upon which the conclusions were based. Psychologist Abraham Maslow criticized the use of volunteers in the studies, saying they skewed the results.

Nevertheless, *Sexual Behavior in the Human Male* was touted in the media as the "raciest" sex book ever to hit American bookstores. *Sexual Behavior in the Human Female* came out five years later in 1953. The overall theme: sexual liberation, with marriage downgraded and trivialized. The warped corollary: The sex offender is not a monster— just someone who is not very different from others in his social group and whose behavior is probably similar to others in his community, but who have not yet gotten into trouble on account of their inclinations or who, at least, have not gone as far in indulging them as he has!

## Kinsey's impact on society

Kinsey co-author Dr. Wardell Pomeroy wrote a 1972 memoir about his boss and the Institute. It contains a remarkable story which reveals how the Rockefeller Foundation viewed Kinsey's impact:

> *In 1963 when the foundation was celebrating its*

*50th anniversary, (Indiana University President Herman) Wells was among the 600 guests at a dinner in the Plaza Hotel in New York. (Secretary of State Dean) Rusk was the principal speaker, the Rockefeller family was present, and the guest list included, among others, university presidents and scientists from all over the world. Robert Sproul, who had recently retired as president of the University of California, sat next to Wells, and as the two men chatted amiably together, Wells inquired, "Do you know why we're here, Bob?" Sproul said he assumed it was because their universities had been involved with research grants which the foundation made and considered important.*

*After dinner, Wells repeated this conversation to Dr. Robert S. Morison, head of the medical division of the foundation. "Yes," Morison agreed, "I can tell you exactly why you are here." He went on to relate that each division had been asked to look over its records for the 50 years and determine what grants had been most significant.*

*A young assistant in Morison's division had brought him the Institute records and inquired, "Dr. Morrison, just what is the significance of this?" On his desk that morning Morison happened to have the newest and best gynecology book for medical students. He turned to a chapter and said, "Look here," and then went on to another chapter and still another. "Young man," he said, "this is pure Kinsey. It couldn't have been written before Kinsey, and it has profoundly affected this branch of medicine." After relating the anecdote, Morison said to Wells, "You're here because we consider the Institute financing one of the most significant things we ever did."*

Pomeroy was open about what he described as the Institute's and the Rockefeller Foundation's "grand scheme" of moving from a traditional standard of sexual morality based upon the marriage of a

133

man and woman to one based on simply "free love." Reisman, by the way, tracked the career of Pomeroy, who later became an academic dean at The Sex and Drug Forum (now the Institute for the Advanced Study of Human Sexuality). This is Reisman's description of that organization:

> *Now the leading institution in the sexology field (controlling conference selections, journal publications, lectures, etc.), IASHS has trained more than 100,000 sex educators, doctors and "safe sex" instructors. IASHS is a Kinseyian filter through which almost all "accredited" persons in the sexuality field are screened at some point during their careers. The more formal course work includes such topics as "erotic sensate and massage therapy" ... and teaching students how to give expert-witness court testimony favoring obscenity, pornography and reduced penalties for sex crimes.*

When the Reece Committee was probing foundations in 1953-54, the Kinsey Institute became one of the grantees it proposed to most intensely scrutinize. That's when panel members really began to feel the heat from the rest of Congress, the Eisenhower administration and the media. Committee Counsel Rene Wormser in *The Foundations: Their Power and Influence* recalls in particular "the unreasoning opposition" of U.S. Rep. Wayne Hayes, D-Ohio, "who threatened to fight against the appropriation (to the Committee) on the floor of the House unless the Kinsey investigation (was) dropped."

The "invisible government" had stepped in to protect a sacred cow, so the Reece Committee's days were numbered. Even so, the panel issued a warning describing the philosophy of "social scientists" seeking to change America:

> *...That there are no absolutes, that everything is indeterminate, that no standards of conduct, morals, ethics and government are to be deemed inviolate, that everything, including basic moral law, is subject to change, and that it is the part of the social scientists to*

*take no principle for granted as a premise in social or juridical reasoning, however fundamental it may hereto have been deemed to be under our Judeo-Christian moral system.*

Having dodged congressional exposure, the Rockefeller Foundation nonetheless ended donations to the Kinsey Institute in 1954. Then-president Rusk redirected grants, instead, to the American Law Institute for creation of a revolutionary new "model penal code." Funding the Kinsey Institute was no longer necessary, because its mentor— basking in a reputation as the nation's foremost scientific authority on human sexuality— already had published a great body of work on his subject. The Rockefeller mission was complete. Kinsey's studies would be the basis for the new code, so the doctor could be tossed aside.

## Widespread legal impact

American Civil Liberties Union attorney Morris Ernest, whose clients included Kinsey, Kinsey's Institute and later the Sex Information and Education Council of the United States, wrote a revealing book in 1948 titled *American Sexual Behavior and the Kinsey Report.* The ACLU lawyer quoted Kinsey associate Robert Dickinson as saying that "an era of hush-and-pretend in the life of our nation may end" through publication of *Sexual Behavior of the Human Male* and that "virtually every page of the *Kinsey Report* touches on some section of the legal code ... a reminder that the law, like ... our social pattern, falls lamentably short of being based on a knowledge of facts."

Retired Marine Col. Ronald Ray, in a column "Kinsey's Legal Legacy" in the Jan. 19, 1998 issue of *The New American*, chronicles what came next:

> *Ernest advised that every bar association in the country 'should establish a Committee on the Law of Sexual Behavior and consider its own state's legal system in this field...' Soon Committees were*

135

*established with funding from the Rockefeller Foundation in an effort to overturn the American way of life.*

*In 1955, the Model Penal Code was completed under the auspices of the Carnegie— and Rockefeller — seeded American Law Institute, the education arm of the American Bar Association. This 'model' was then submitted to state legislatures for their consideration, with plenty of authoritative support for its implementation provided by Kinsey's flawed scientific analysis. Adoption of the Model Penal Code eliminated and/or trivialized prior sex offenses, eventually aiding the reduction of penalties for abortion, rape, wife and child battery, desertion, seduction, adultery, prostitution, contributing to the delinquency of a minor, soliciting for masturbation, sodomy, public sexual exhibitions, 'unfit' parentage, alienation of affection, and obscenity, as well as infanticide, premeditated AIDS/STD transmission, etc.*

America's common law was indeed gradually supplanted. Rape not so long ago was punishable by death in about half of the states, yet Kinsey's data was used to justify ending capital punishment for that crime (a trend which even irked some feminists). Since his studies "found" a majority of women to be promiscuous, adultery laws were naturally weakened (along with the awarding of alimony to an abandoned wife). In the decades since Kinsey's death, numerous court cases have cited his research. Liberal U.S. Supreme Court justices began quoting Kinsey in their opinions. Statutes criminalizing unconventional sexual activity have been ruled "unconstitutional" based on Kinsey data. In a 1973 Tennessee case, for instance, a judge quoted Kinsey to argue that sodomy "is approved by almost 90 percent of adults between 18 and 34." To deem it a crime, the judge said, "would seem to me to be judicial legislation of the plainest kind."

Author Ray believes the use of Kinsey's data in the courts may be viewed as "a contributing factor to the current exhaustion of our criminal justice system." Indeed, the increasing early release of murderers, rapists and child predators back into society underscore an amoral system in chaos.

Consider the "diversity" ramifications of the 1987 District of Columbia case *Gay Rights Coalition v. Georgetown University*. The court nauseatingly cited "the Kinsey scale" in ruling that the Christian-oriented college must recognize a homosexual student club:

> *From Kinsey's study of 12,000 white males, still the largest of its kind, Kinsey reported that only 50 percent had neither overt nor psychic homosexual experiences after the onset of adolescence. Another 37 percent had at least some overt homosexual experience to the point of orgasm between adolescence and old age, while the remaining 13 percent reacted erotically to other males without having physical contacts. Almost half of his sample had both heterosexual and homosexual experiences at some point in their lives.*

> *Kinsey's findings challenged the popular assumption that the vast majority of people are either exclusively heterosexual or exclusively homosexual and suggested that instead individual sexual responses and behavior fall somewhere between extremes for some 46 percent of the population. While stressing the existence of a continuum, for convenience Kinsey adopted a seven-point scale, with zero denoting the exclusively homosexual and six the exclusively heterosexual. The Kinsey scale continues to be relied upon today ... At a minimum, Kinsey's research claimed a diversity of human sexual orientations.*

"America's original dirty old man" would have reveled in what he has wrought. Consider just one slice of current American life—typical daytime television soap operas. They contain almost every aspect of Kinsey's "anything goes" philosophy.

# Foundation-funded sexology

After the death of Kinsey, wealthy foundations assisted in spreading his "enlightened" values-neutral sex education nationwide. In 1964 the Kinsey Institute launched the Sex Information and Education Council of the United States (SIECUS), first headed by Kinsey disciple Dr. Mary Calderone. It later changed its name to the Sexuality Information and Education Council of the United States. The Playboy Foundation, run by *Playboy* magazine founder Hugh Hefner, provided the original seed money for SIECUS and Kinsey colleague Pomeroy was among its first board members.

SIECUS grants in recent years come from the William and Flora Hewlett Foundation, the Buffett Foundation, the Ford Foundation, the Summit Foundation, the David and Lucille Packard Foundation, the John D. and Catherine T. MacArthur Foundation, the Charles Stewart Mott Foundation, the Moriah Fund, the Jessie Smith Noyes Foundation, the Public Welfare Foundation, the George Gund Foundation, the Carnegie Corporation of New York, the Robert Sterling Clark Foundation, the Compton Foundation, the Geraldine R. Dodge Foundation, the Kaiser Family Fund and the Turner Foundation.

It would take volumes to analyze all the propaganda in various forms that SIECUS has poured into public schools and elsewhere. Suffice it to say that the common message is a downgrading of marriage, encouragement of teen condom use and criticism of abstinence-only-before-marriage sex education policies funded by the federal government and adhered to by a majority of states. A Hewlett grant paid for a particularly vicious piece of propaganda— a "documentary" movie called "The Education of Shelby Knox." It features a self-described 15-year-old Baptist girl who becomes a "comprehensive sex education" advocate after rejecting her Lubbock, Texas, school system's abstinence-only-before-marriage curriculum. (In 2006 the film won a Council on Foundations "excellence" award, was featured at the 2005 Sundance Festival and was aired nationwide on the left-leaning Public Broadcasting System.)

A 1996 *SIECUS Report* typically urged use of "sexually explicit visual, printed or on-line materials" for school children to "reduce ignorance and confusion." *Time*— never accused of being politically conservative— once reported on a SIECUS paper titled "Attacking the Last Taboo." The paper proclaimed, "We are roughly in the same position today regarding incest as we were 100 years ago with respect to our fears of masturbation." The April 14, 1980 issue of *Time* accurately tagged SIECUS as part of a "pro-incest lobby."

Pornography has been around since ancient times but, post-Kinsey, top-selling adult publications— often dismissed simply as "girlie" magazines— are featuring more child exploitation. Dr. Judith Reisman again emerges as one of the "good guys" contributing to scholarly research in this area. She served as the principal investigator for an extensive 1984-85 study "Children, Crime and Violence in the Pictorial Imagery of *Playboy, Penthouse* and *Hustler*," compiled at American University and funded through the U.S. Justice Department.

Visual images of children in sexual and violent contexts were analyzed in 683 issues of those three adult magazines beginning with *Playboy*'s initial December 1953 issue through *Playboy, Penthouse* and *Hustler* issues of December 1984. It is astounding to analyze the study's findings. A total of 6,004 photographs, illustrations and cartoons depicting children appeared in the 683 magazines. One of the study's conclusions: "Almost all depictions of child sexual abuse portrayed the child as unharmed or benefited by the activity." Now, of course, the Internet is a nirvana for sex deviants interested in children under the age of 18.

A particularly extreme example of "Kinsey gone wild" occurred in New York in 1995 when state authorities agreed that the North American Man/Boy Love Association, despite a patently immoral agenda which seeks to legitimize pedophilia, could operate as a legitimate non-profit organization entitled to receive charitable donations and taxpayer-financed grants. NAMBLA, which advocates elimination of sexual age-of-consent laws, has been defended by the ACLU in court on "free speech" grounds— even though ACLU Massachusetts director John Reinstein admitted the group "may extol conduct which is currently illegal."

# Abortion ... and more

Promotion of abortion as a form of birth control in the 1960s and '70s was a priority for the Rockefeller and Ford foundations, and later by the Hewlett Foundation and others as revealed by their federal tax 990 forms. After the 1973 *Roe v. Wade* U.S. Supreme Court ruling, in which Justice Harry Blackmun infamously wrote that "the word person, as used in the 14th Amendment, does not include the unborn," all kinds of programs to limit the American population through abortion were undertaken. A June 2, 1972 *Chicago Tribune* story contained this gem: "It is no surprise that Playboy Foundation money is now competing with Rockefeller money to promote the concept of permissive abortion." The March 31, 1973 *Indianapolis News* summarized how the super-rich liberal elites viewed the high court's sweeping ruling:

> *Now that the Supreme Court has legalized abortion, says Dr. John Knowles, president of the Rockefeller Foundation, government at all levels should get busy and see to it they are performed as quickly and cheaply as possible. The free market, he asserts, is okay for soap and automobiles, but abortion should be a matter for government.*

John D. Rockefeller III, in fact, once headed a federal commission which recommended not only taxpayer-financed abortion (regardless of anyone's religious objections) but the teaching of abortion psychology in public schools and colleges.

The Washington-D.C.-based National Association for the Repeal of Abortion Laws— NARAL Pro Choice America— was born in 1969 and is the largest of the abortion cheerleaders, coordinating thousands of activists nationwide. The group opposes banning of the gruesome, third trimester procedure known as partial birth abortion. It even unsuccessfully opposed passage of a 2004 law that recognizes unborn babies as crime victims when they die as a result of a violent crime against an expectant mother.

Through its parallel political action committee, NARAL conducts voter turnout drives, publishes voter guides, launches public relations campaigns and targets pro-life politicians for defeat. (In the 2004 election cycle, it contributed $430,750 to Democratic candidates and $10,000 to Republicans.) Most of the foundations listed in chapter four, as well as many others, are contributors to this tax-exempt 501(c)(3) operation.

The Ford Foundation funds an extensive pro-abortion network in the U.S. and around the world through programs euphemistically listed on its website as "Asset Building and Community Development" and "Knowledge, Creativity and Freedom." Just one of several radical groups receiving millions of Ford dollars in recent years is the Washington, D.C.-based Catholics for Free Choice, which constantly challenges the pro-life orthodoxy of the Roman Catholic Church. In 2003, for instance, the group demanded that the European Union repeal permission for Catholic hospitals and schools to use EU funds without being required to follow "diversity" rules that would force them to hire gays, divorced people and pro-abortionists. A flattering article on the group in the Feb. 27 *New York Times* said "the constant refrain in this office is, 'Are we really Catholic?'" Why a wholly secular foundation should involve itself in a major doctrinal dispute within the world's largest Christian church organization by bankrolling one side is not readily apparent. Such a secularist intrusion into church affairs clearly violates the spirit if not the letter of the principle of separation of church and state.

A relatively new cause— acceptance of homosexuality as a lifestyle— has garnered ardent foundation support. The Funders for Lesbian and Gay Issues was established in 1982 to help spearhead "gay rights" in the political and cultural arena. Ford was among a handful of foundation contributors that year. Twenty years later, according to the group's annual report, "139 foundations awarded 1,500 grants totaling $30 million in support of lesbian, gay, bisexual and transgender issues and organizations." The report glowingly added "marriage and civil unions is the issue receiving the largest percentage of funding to the field."

In bed with SIECUS and the National Education Association (NEA) is the New York City-based Gay, Lesbian and Straight Education Network (GLSEN). It distributes the usual propaganda, especially targeting elementary school students, and promotes a book *Celebrating Families* that features lesbians with adopted daughters. In 1999 GLSEN's then-communications director confidently predicted that "we're going to raise a generation of kids who don't believe the religious right." Its Annual Report indicates that major 2005 funders include the Ford, Snowden and Gill foundations, some corporations and— you guessed it— the NEA.

Dozens of leftist foundations give in varying degrees to a growing number of lesbian, gay, bisexual and transgender groups. The David Geffen Foundation, based in Universal City, Ca., and headed by the well-known Hollywood billionaire, has emerged in recent years as a major underwriter of influential ones— especially the Gay and Lesbian Alliance Against Defamation and the National Gay and Lesbian Task Force both based in Los Angeles. The New York City-based Gay Men's Health Crisis also enjoys a variety of big donors, ranging from the AT&T Foundation to the Samuel Bronfman Foundation.

# WHAT IS TO BE DONE?
## CHAPTER VIII

*"Of every thousand dollars spent in so-called charity today, it is possible that $950 is unwisely spent; so spent, indeed as to produce the very evils which it proposes to mitigate or cure." – Andrew Carnegie, 1889.*

A common perception is that corporate wealth— a symbol of "capitalism"— tilts toward the political right. Liberals love to throw around "Halliburton" as a leading villain of corporate infamy (although the Clinton administration was just as friendly to Dick Cheney's old corporation as the Bush administration). Is this accurate?

The Washington, D.C.-based Capital Research Center recently undertook an analysis of Fortune 500 companies operating non-profit charitable foundations that donate to groups on the left and right. Nonprofits on the "right" were defined as favoring lower taxes, less government regulation, less governmental spending on social programs but more on defense. The Center designated as "right" those groups defending traditional values, the right to bear arms, tougher laws against criminals and tighter restrictions on immigration. "Left" nonprofits were categorized as advocating higher taxes in order to spend more on social programs even as defense spending is reduced, tighter gun control laws, less restrictive immigration laws and, generally speaking, more lenient criminal laws. The Center also tabulated grants across the spectrum to leftist outfits like the Natural Resources Defense Council and to conservative groups like the National Right to Life Committee.

What was the result? An examination of the foundations' IRS 990 forms, and a compilation of the dollar values for grants and matching grants to left-wing and right-wing groups, reveals the left getting far more money.

The left received nearly $59 million while the right garnered about $4 million, a ratio of 14.5 to 1. The Center said "even if we subtract a single $35 million mega-grant from the Goldman Sachs Foundation to the liberal Wildlife Conservation Society, donations to the left still outstrip those to the right by a ratio of 5.8 to 1."

Another indicator of the growing power of left-wing grantmaking is evident from an examination of the activities of groups known as 527s, named after a section of the IRS Code. They are private non-profits designed to promote political candidates and causes. They take foundation funds and unlimited so-called 'soft" money, and they are less regulated than other non-profits engaged in electioneering. In giving to these groups, the left again far outstrips conservative giving.

"Thus far in 2006, 17 of the top 25 contributors to 527 advocacy groups are funding liberal/Democratic causes, including liberal billionaires George Soros and Peter Lewis," writes Peter Schweizer in the Oct. 30, 2006 *National Review.* In 2004 Schweizer found Democrats made up 15 of the 25 individuals who gave more than $2 million to 527 groups. The GOP, Schweizer finds, is largely a party funded by middle-class voters.

Consider, too, these discoveries courtesy of journalist Michael Barone: Democratic 2004 presidential candidate John Kerry won only one county in Idaho— the Sun Valley home of the super-rich. He carried only one Wyoming county— the one including wealthy Jackson Hole. Why is this? Perhaps the main reason is that wealth is amassed quickly by most Hollywood and high-tech tycoons. This author has interviewed age 30-something entrepreneurs who have a totally different outlook on wealth than do traditional captains of industry who labored a lifetime, and who overcame governmental barriers, before they were able to accumulate their fortunes. These younger tycoons are more liberal politically, so the ranks of the super-rich left are growing. And they are using foundations and now 527s not to primarily help the less fortunate but to politically transform the United States.

## Time for accountability

Joel Fleishman in *The Foundation: A Great American Secret* says:

> *U.S. taxpayers annually benefit U.S. foundations with forgone taxes in excess of $20 billion. For that reason alone, foundations must somehow be made accountable, preferably by means of voluntary action but, failing that, through legally mandated regulation ...*

In this vein, Rick Cohen, executive director of the National Committee for Responsive Philanthropy, notes that:

> *Like any sector of our economy or society, change occurs when it is penetrated by constituents, consumers, citizens asking for something better than the deal they are being dealt. Philanthropy can aim to do much better on these items, but it won't unless the nonprofit sector— the delivery system without which the tax-exempt value of philanthropy could not and would not be realized— realizes that it is their right and responsibility to demand a different kind of philanthropy from the nation's foundations.*

Author and journalism professor Marvin Olasky expands on Cohen's point, reminding us that the promotion of a leftist ideological agenda by foundations, especially promotion of bigger and more regulated government, has been a huge waste:

> *Two decades of site visits have shown me that governmental bureaucracy is hazardous to community health, and that churches can build bonds of attachment far stronger than the gossamer chords cut from parachutes of dropped-off activists. Sadly, American philanthropy over the past 50 years has often been pro-government and, in practice if not necessarily in philosophy, anti-church (unless the churches have become government look-alikes).*

Frenchman Alexis de Tocqueville, when touring America in the 1840s, witnessed the young country's strength through local churches and voluntary community associations. He chronicled that they were important catalysts prodding people into being better citizens. Yet William A. Schambra, director of the Hudson Institute's Bradley Center for Philanthropy and Civic Renewal, rightly notes that America's first large foundations were run by "progressive intellectuals" who "dismissed America's small, local civic associations as petty, parochial, outdated relics of the past, doomed by vast, new, community-shattering social forces like urbanization and industrialization." Their political elites "steeped in social science expertise," Schambra writes, thought they would be "able to harness forces for the good" once power was centralized in Washington, D.C., and away from the local level. He further asks:

> *A number of concerns are raised by this view of philanthropy, not the least of which is: after billions of philanthropic dollars spent over the course of a century getting at 'root causes,' has even one significant social problem been traced to its roots and 'conquered' once and for all?*

That's an interesting question. Whatever one's answer, Schambra addresses the heart of the problem: Today's foundation leftists "steeped in the social sciences" would be Tocqueville's worst nightmare. "The gradual accumulation of authority in the hands of expert elites, happy to solve problems for people so long as they are left 'free from constraints,'" Schambra says, "is precisely the danger he feared above all in the age of democracy."

This lack of overall accountability— and the fact that leftists use it successfully for their own ends— should outrage all intellectually honest Americans.

## Steps toward reform

President Trent Stamp of Charity Navigator, on the Internet at www.charitynavigator.com, chides the non-profit sector for "evading the reformer's axe." His group serves as an effective *Consumer Reports*-type watchdog, with its website explaining that it "compares organizations' finances with their peers, who are competing with them for the dollars of those donors who believe that their cause is one of merit." Charity Navigator has a rating system so one can check which non-profits are operating efficiently, which ones are top-heavy with administration, which ones have efficient fund-raising operations, etc. Stamp, in his essays, asks tough questions like "what's wrong with a minimum program expense ratio requirement?" (Why shouldn't American taxpayers demand, for example, that charities spend half of what they raise on their programs?) He also asks "what's wrong with reporting your single entry organization as a single entity?" (Such a rule would hurt many left-wing foundations, which use the ruse to hide costs and expenses.)

The Independent Sector is a Washington, D.C.-based coalition of foundations, corporations and private voluntary groups that work to strengthen U.S. non-profits. It convened a Panel on the Non-profit Sector and later issued 29 "draft principles" to improve foundation governance, board financial oversight and fundraising practices. Since the Panel on the Non-profit Sector and Charity Navigator are helping to foster a reform debate, consider these wide-ranging proposed courses of action:

- There are new models and approaches even liberal foundation boards could adopt. Some non-profits are achieving success, for example, with reforming and streamlining, rather than expanding, government. Some assist viable private alternatives to public (i.e. government) schools. The Northwest Area Foundation, to cite another example, helps communities reduce poverty by identifying, sharing and advocating what works— not for governments but for the local populace. President Karl N. Stauber says Northwest "no longer sees itself as a grantmaker, with non-profits as it primary customer." Instead, he says, "it invests resources to create new knowledge that communities can apply to reducing poverty." By going directly to the local level, Stauber adds, "the foundation does not ask the federal government to 'bless' or support its actions." Some left-wingers are taking note. At a 2005 New York Regional Association of Grantmakers conference, two environmentalist speakers said left-"progressives" needed to abandon issue-based advocacy and instead search for "bridge values" to build new coalitions. "That's tough advice to give to a bunch of rigid ideologues," *Philanthropy Notes* observed.

- Foundations that don't want to see their original charitable mission or donor intent subverted by future presidents or trustees sometimes choose to eventually shut down, with accelerated spending on the key goals. The Irene and Aaron Diamond Foundation, Atlantic Philanthropies and the John M. Olin Foundation are examples. Or, foundations can redouble efforts at vigilance and legal protection. In 2005, *Philanthropy Notes* reported that Sir John Templeton passed control of the billion-dollar Templeton Foundation to his 65-year-old son. "Sir John takes donor intent seriously," *Notes* said, because "future foundation officers will have to read his articles and books, and every five years three independent analysts will conduct a review of the foundation's work to ensure it is making grants consistent with Templeton's intent." Furthermore, if the analysts find that the son is giving 9 percent of the grants to causes inconsistent with his father's conservative Christian intentions, the heir has one year to bring the grants back into line or he and his two top aides will be automatically fired. If only more foundation pioneers in the 20th century had thought of that!

• Americans have a right to know— to some extent — what foundations, and the non-profits they fund, are doing. Remember that many tax-exempt entities as noted in the first chapter have become pass-through operations that shield the identity of the original donor of the grant and which publicize only the name of the eventual recipient. This is a game of earmarking a gift for a precise project or organization by funneling it though a foundation which redirects it to an often more radical third party. In foundation-speak, these are "donor-advised funds." If the IRS won't do a better auditing and policing job with regard to these and other abuses, a suggestion comes from Marcus Owens, former head of the IRS Exempt Organization Division. He advocates creation of a congressionally chartered, private not-for-profit independent organization to coordinate with the understaffed IRS on legal and ethical oversight. It would be modeled on the National Association of Security Dealers (NASD), which oversees brokers and, of course, would require appropriate funding, manpower and resources to be effective. But there are dangers in creating such an entity, as articulated by The Philanthropy Roundtable at the end of this chapter.

- Educating the public, including voters, on public policy issues— even with a spin— is fine. But a federal and state crackdown on blatant foundation political activity and illegal lobbying is long overdue. As the president of a 501(c)(3) foundation, I have had to be mindful about lobbying for a particular piece of legislation and extremely careful that no partisan bias be displayed (as opposed to airing a politically philosophical point of view). In recent decades, the IRS has had little incentive to spend time on foundation abuses, since its personnel have had far bigger financial fish to fry. During the Clinton administration, though, a blatant double standard emerged. IRS bureaucrats threatened the tax-exempt status of several conservative foundations for alleged partisanship. Countless hours and dollars were wasted over several years in complying with investigators' demands for paperwork, and nothing unlawful was found. Under that administration as well as the current Bush presidency, left-wing violators have had no fear of the IRS. (Consider one example: the League of Conservation Voters, a self-admitted member of "the shadow Democratic Party." By its own description, it "helped hundreds of environmental leaders to victory, both on Capitol Hill and at the ballot box.") Flagrant partisan and electoral advocacy— either from the left or right— should result in swift removal of a foundation's tax-exempt status.

- All 50 states through their attorneys general could exercise a more forceful oversight and enforcement role. Michigan's attorney general, as noted in the third chapter, is using administrative subpoenas and the state's charitable trust laws to ascertain whether the Ford Foundation is, in his words, "running a tight ship" and renewing its obligation to original donor intent. In an April 2, 2006 *Detroit*

*News* column on the Michigan investigation, Daniel Howes noted:

*Unhappy donors are raising questions, sometimes with lawsuits against such heavyweights as Princeton University, over how institutions are administering their gifts. And at least one attorney general, in Missouri, two years ago used his powers to force change at the Ewing Marion Kauffman Foundation.*

New York, California and Massachusetts have also been aggressive with regard to non-profit abuse and illegalities by trustees and staffers.

- A coalition of Democrats and Republicans in Congress concerned about the foundations' competing "invisible government" agenda should initiate a dual strategy: 1) greater oversight over the questionable activities of foundations in the political realm; and, 2) the enactment of narrowly-tailored legislation to curb abuses.

## What Congress could do

Why shouldn't Congress insist that these incorporated endowments pay full corporate taxes and end political activities? If they are to be tax-free, shouldn't they be responsible to a public whose taxes carry the load they are shirking? Why not require that they spend half of what they raise on programs that are indisputably in the broad public interest? How about ending the charade of a "single entity" that is in reality several foundations sharing the same address, office and staff?

The Reece Committee concluded that, unlike corporate structures, foundations are "unchecked by stockholders"; unlike government they are "unchecked by the people"; and unlike churches they are "unchecked by any firmly established canons of value." That is still true, which is why Fleishman offers national lawmakers a modest starting point for reform: Enact a separate Freedom of Information Act requiring foundations to make public all documents generated in the process of making a grant above a specific dollar amount. The proposed statute would include public charities that were once private foundations. A foundation will not infrequently carry out a disguised partisan political program under a "front group" name which hides the true source of funding for the project. Such deceit is wholly inconsistent with the purposes for which foundations were granted favored status under the tax laws and should be made illegal.

Charity Navigator's Stamp poses the following question which is also extremely pertinent to the manner in which foundations conduct their affairs:

> *Should charities really be allowed to do financial business with family members? Why are charities, which are tax-exempt and chartered to serve the public good, allowed to reward multi-million contracts without a competitive or open bidding process? All local governments are forbidden from these types of practices. Why do we demand less from our non-profits?*

If Congress ever gets the spine to implement comprehensive foundation reform, Stamp further recommends that stringent requirements be enacted governing the creation of new foundations for the following reasons:

> *Every time a natural disaster happens, amateurs race to incorporate new non-profits, as if the currently existing ones weren't up to the task. And if the cause is politically popular enough...the IRS actually moves these groups to the front of the line for approval. Why should we make it easier for people who have never done this kind of work and were never moved to entertain the idea before to enter the space and compete with reputable, experienced*

*organizations, especially when we know from experience that most of the newcomers will simply fail?*

## Gates Foundation shows promise

Amid the calls for foundation reform, there is cause for hope with the working model of the world's biggest charitable organization, the Bill and Melinda Gates Foundation. Far-left foundations will be around for a long time and new ones will bloom, but the example by Bill and Melinda Gates is resonating throughout the philanthropic world.

Gates announced he will leave as Microsoft's CEO, probably in 2008, to devote full attention to world health issues and improving U.S. education, partly by establishing charter and private schools. He is mightily assisted by Warren Buffett's $31 billion gift. To put it in perspective, the $1.36 billion spent by the Gates Foundation in 2005 closely approximates the entire World Health Organization budget for that same year.

Terrence Scanlon of the Capital Research Center, in an August 2006 article "Buffett's Compassionate Calling," writes:

> *By giving to the Gates Foundation, Buffett acknowledges and accepts its priorities, which are curing and preventing diseases that afflict the world's poor and improving American education. Recent articles about the Gates Foundation say its approach to these problems is encouraging. The foundation is a streamlined organization that, like any good businessperson, holds accountable those who receive its grants and demands measurable outcomes, not vague promises.*

Scanlon, whose Center is a premier foundation watchdog, feels the Microsoft wizard— while giving relatively small amounts to liberal groups— "seems more interested in getting things done, solving real problems that are fundamentally nonpolitical." He also believes that Melinda Gates, raised as a Roman Catholic, "should be credited with reorienting her husband's— and Warren Buffett's— thinking about how to help the world's poor by curing disease rather than by fighting overpopulation."

Ford and the other top left-wing foundations, of course, will continue to aggressively push their agenda in the U.S. and around the globe. But the world of philanthropy, for the first time in a long time, is confronted with a stark contrast. There are two competing worldviews now— the hard left model typified by Ford and the Gates approach.

The biggest danger? Leftists or family members will seek to hijack the Gates Foundation or derail its current mission, either while Gates and Buffett are alive or after their passing. Irwin Stelzer in the July 17, 2006 *Weekly Standard* fears:

> *(A) hint that history will be repeated at some point comes from the concerns of four foundations that Warren Buffett has set up, three for his children: environmental improvement; educational opportunities for low-income children; human rights; and abortion rights and anti-nuclear proliferation. All laudable, perhaps, but all issues high on the priority list of the liberal establishment.*

The Sept. 18, 2006 issue of *Fortune* reports that the small William J. Clinton Foundation (assets $30 million in 2006), headed by the former president, is trying to make a splash with annual celebrity-attended Global Initiative conferences as well as by teaming up with the Gateses on AIDS work. Former Clinton aide Richard Holbrooke gushingly calls a future hoped-for partnership between the two men "the beginning of what you might call the first super NGO (non-governmental organization)." So far Gates isn't falling into the trap of fully throwing in with Clinton or any other politician or with any traditional left-wing foundation. Gates seems to envision an efficient Microsoft-style, targeted management approach to helping to educate people, to uplifting the poor and to fighting disease— not more of the same discredited big government or United Nations approaches.

# The conservative foundations

While left-wing foundation spending dwarfs that of their politically conservative, free market counterparts, a grantmaking analysis of 12 core foundations on the right reveals growth and promise. A report by the National Committee for Responsive Philanthropy lists the dozen as: the Lynde and Harry Bradley Foundation; the Carthage Foundation; the Earhart Foundation; the Charles G. Koch, David H. Koch and Claude R. Lambe charitable foundations; the Phillip M. McKenna Foundation; the J.M. Foundation; the John M. Olin Foundation; the Henry Salvatori Foundation; the Sarah Scaife Foundation; and the Smith Richardson Foundation.

In 1994 these philanthropies controlled over $1 billion in assets. By 2000 they had donated at least $1 billion since 1985 according to the Media Transparency grants database. Much of this was obviously to support the recipients' policy objectives as well as to expand the right-wing think tank infrastructure. Many grantees, interestingly, pursue an agenda that seeks to transfer authority and responsibility for social welfare from the national government to the charitable sector and to state and local governments.

The National Committee for Responsive Philanthropy report says the 12 targeted the following key sectors:

- *Conservative scholarship programs, training the next generation of thinkers and activists and reverse progressive curricula and policy trends on the nation's college and university campuses.* (The now-closed Olin Foundation, in particular, funded the growth of almost 100 alternative conservative campus newspapers since 1980.)

- *Build and strengthen a national infrastructure of think tanks and advocacy groups ...* (The public relations-savvy Washington, D.C.-based

Heritage Foundation may be the most well-known of these.)

- *Finance alternative media outlets, media watchdog groups and public television and radio for specific, issue-oriented public affairs or news reporting.*

- *Assist conservative pro-market law firms and other law-related projects and organizations.* (Constitutional legal foundations around the nation, often countering the American Civil Liberties Union, have especially grown over the past 25 years. And it was a grant from the Olin Foundation that launched the influential Federalist Society.)

- *Support a network of regional and state-based think tanks and advocacy institutions. Work to transform the social views and giving practices of the nation's religious and philanthropic leaders.*

These 12 foundations as well as other conservative charities have been steadily donating for over 20 years giving them, in the report's words, "a tremendous offensive capacity to influence specific policies and audiences, and also to shape the overall framework in which important fiscal, regulatory and social policy decisions are made."

## A cautionary reform note

The Philanthropy Roundtable, a Washington, D.C.-based association, raises two significant areas of criticism with regard to the Independent Sector's draft principles of self-regulation and overall congressional reform.

156

In an open letter to the Independent Sector, Roundtable President Adam Meyerson writes:

> *First, we fear that some of the draft principles take a 'one-size-fits all' approach to setting rules for a very diverse sector, or would require private organizations to reveal publicly their internal decision-making process.*

> *Second, we are concerned about how the proposed principles would be administered and enforced. Independent Sector doesn't explain what it means by 'self-regulation.' And there are some forms of self-regulation that would be seriously harmful to the foundation world and to charitable giving.*

Meyerson, a former Heritage Foundation vice president, notes the Roundtable would "strongly oppose the creation of a new industry-wide rule-making and enforcement agency modeled on the NASDF" (as Fleishman proposes). He makes several cogent points in his letter: 1) Over-regulation can be just as great under private as well as under public rule-making and enforcement bodies. 2) Creation of a NASDF-like self-regulation entity amounts to double taxation. Foundations, Meyerson notes, already pay an excise tax that is supposed to provide the IRS with revenue to police the tax-exempt sector. Foundations would have to pay a second time to a new regulatory body. 3) Since the culture of the IRS is dedicated to protecting the privacy of those it is investigating, that protection "could well be lost" if enforcement were delegated to another regulatory body.

Meyerson issues a final warning:

> *...Creation of a self-regulating body could encourage cartel-like behavior— the use of the rule-making process by politically powerful existing philanthropic leaders to exclude competition from new entrants. This is not an idle threat. Already prominent nonprofit leaders have made proposals to abolish foundations with small asset sizes, or to require family*

157

*foundations to have independent directors. Creation of*
*a new regulatory agency, especially one controlled by*
*the industry, would provide a vehicle for enacting such*
*rules.*

Indeed, it may be best for Congress to pass strict, narrowly tailored reform legislation that would just make the IRS a far more vigorous and objective policeman of abuses, which overwhelmingly occur on the left. In any event, as the left-right cultural war in America continues, both old and new philanthropists— no matter their ideology— would do well to reflect on the ruminations of Andrew Carnegie who counseled over a century ago:

> *These who, would administer wisely must,*
> *indeed, be wise, for one of the most serious obstacles to*
> *the improvement of our race is indiscriminate charity.*
> *It were better for mankind that the millions of the rich*
> *were thrown into the sea than so spent as to encourage*
> *the slothful, the drunken, the unworthy.*

# SELECTED BIBLIOGRAPHY

Allen, Gary. "Foundations: Swindle, Treason and Dodge," *American Opinion.* (Belmont Mass.) November 1969.

Allen, Gary. "Think Tanks." *American Opinion.* (Belmont, Mass.) March 1971.

Arnold, Ron. "The Heinz Foundations and the Kerry Campaign." *Foundation Watch.* (Washington, D.C.) April 2004.

Arnold, Ron. "The Pew Charitable Trusts. Global Warming Power Nexus." *Foundation Watch.* (Washington, D.C.) May 2004.

Arnold, Ron. "The Rockefeller Family Fund: Puppet Master for Leftist Front Groups." *Foundation Watch.* (Washington, D.C.) January 2005.

Babbitt, Bruce. *Cities in the Wilderness: A New Vision of Land Use in America.* (Island Press) 2003.

Baldwin, William. "When Ducks Trample Your Liberties." *Forbes.* September 30, 2002.

Banerjee, Neela. "Backing Abortion Rights While Keeping the Faith. A Career Defying Catholic Tenets on Sex." *The New York Times.* February 27, 2007.

Barrett, William P. "The March of the 400." *Forbes.* September 30, 2002.

Beatty, Sally. "Ford Foundation's President Will Retire in 2008." *The Wall Street Journal*. Sept.30-Oct. 1, 2006.

Berlau, John. *Ecofreaks: Environmentalism Is Hazardous to Your Health*. Nelson Current. (Nashville, Tenn.) 2006.

Blunt, Sheryl Henderson. "Cool on Climate Change. New Christian Coalition Says Fighting Global Warming Will Hurt the Poor." *Christianity Today*. September 26, 2006.

Blunt, Sheryl Henderson. "The New Climate Coalition. Evangelical Leaders Bolster the Fight Against Global Warming." *Christianity Today*. February 8, 2006.

Carton, Bob. "Spann Spawns Cyber-Storm." *The Birmingham News*. January 20, 2007.

Chapa, Rebecca. "How Religious Beliefs Shape Today's Issues." *Atlanta Journal-Constitution*. December 18, 2006.

Charen, Mona. "Corporate Purr-meter." *The Washington Times*. June 20, 2001.

Chivian, Eric. "Science Fiction." *Harvard Medical Alumni Bulletin*. Spring 2005.

Cooperman, Alan. "Christian Groups Spar Over Funding. Support Sources Called Political." *The Washington Post*. January 12, 2007.

Cooperman, Alan. "Evangelicals Broaden Their Moral Agenda." *Washington Post*. October 19, 2006.

Crichton. Michael. *State of Fear*. (Harper Collins) 2004.

Dew, Diane. "Who Funds Homosexual and Lesbian Groups." The Foundation Center. October 2000.

Evans, Christopher. "Conservative Spotlight: DiscovertheNetworks.org." *Human Events*. July 4, 2005.

Hollis, Ernest V. *Philanthropic Foundations and Higher Education.* (Columbia University Press.) 1938.

Howes, Daniel. "Ford Foundation Probed; AG claims Michigan Left Out." *Detroit News.* April 2, 2006.

Howes, Daniel. "Hometown Gleans Ford Foundation Funds Again." *The Detroit News.* February 2, 2007.

Fleishman, Joel. *The Foundation: A Great American Secret.* Public Affairs. (New York). 2007.

Forbes, Steve. "Term Limits for Foundations." *Forbes.* July 24, 2006.

Fosdick, Raymond. *The Story of the Rockefeller Foundation.* Harper and Brothers. (New York) 1963.

Gannon, Francis X. *Biographical Dictionary of the Left. (Consolidated Vol. I).* Western Islands. 1969.

Goldstein, Lorrie. "The Kyoto Horror Show." *Toronto Sun.* February 18, 2007.

Henninger, Daniel. "Giving Wisely." *The Wall Street Journal.* July 14, 2006.

Hogberg, David & Haney, Sarah. "Funding Liberalism With Blue-Chip Profits: Fortune 100 Foundations Back Leftist Causes." *Foundation Watch.* (Washington, D.C.) August 2006.

"Inflexible Fence Could Spell Disaster for Southwest Wildlife." PPN Online. (Non-profit News and Information.) October 27, 2006.

Johnson, Ben. "Charitable' Foundations: ATMS for the Left." FrontPageMagazine.com. March 2, 2004.

Johnson, Ben. "Who's Behind the Immigration Rallies?" FrontPageMagazine.com. March 29, 2006.

Johnson, Jeff. "Turner: Murdoch Is the World's Most Dangerous Man." NewsMax.com (West Palm Beach, Fla.) July 2003.

Jones, James. *Alfred C. Kinsey: A Public/Private Life*. (W.W. Norton & Co.) 1997.

Kersten, Katherine. "Environmentalists Have Embarked on a Secular Crusade." *Minneapolis Star-Tribune*. February 7, 2007.

Kinsey, Alfred, Wardell Pomeroy and Martin, Clyde. *Sexual Behavior in the Human Male*. W.B. Saunders. (Philadelphia, Pa.) 1948.

Kratz, Ellen Florian & Burke, Doris. "An Almanac of American Wealth." *Fortune*. March 5, 2007.

Kolko, Gabriel. *The Triumph of Conservatism: A Reinterpretation of American History, 1900-1916*. Free Press of Glencoe. 1963.

Lamm, Richard. "For Sale: The Politics of the Sierra Club." *The Social Contract*. (Petoskey, Mich.) Fall 2006.

MacDonald, Heather. "Clinical, Cynical." *The Wall Street Journal*. January 11, 2006.

Maghami, Neil. "The PBS Foundation: Soros Grantec Shields Public TV from Accountability." *Foundation Watch*. February 2007.

Manly, Lorne & Jensen, Elizabeth. "Public TV and Radio to Receive Big Grants." *The New York Times*. May 10, 2005.

McIllhany, William H. *The Tax-Exempt Foundations*. Arlington House. (Westport, Conn.) 1980.

McLean, Bethany. "The Power of Philanthropy." *Fortune*. September 18, 2006.

Miller, John J. "The Politics of Permanent Immigration." *Reason*. October 1998.

Oko, Dan. "Conservation Meets Immigration." HighCountryNews.org. February 18, 2002.

Olasky, Marvin. "Philanthropic Correctness." *Heterodoxy.* October 1992.

Pearce, Jean. "Bill Moyers: Fat Cat for the Fifth Column." FrontPageMagazine.com. March 6, 2003.

Ponte, Lowell. "George Soros: Billionaire for the Left." FrontPageMagazine.com. November 13, 2003.

Ray, Col. Ronald D. Ray. "Kinsey's Legal Legacy," *The New American.* January 19, 1998.

"Report. Special Committee to Investigate Tax-Exempt Foundations." (Reece Committee). December 16, 1954.

Reisman, Dr. Judith A. *Crime & Consequences (Second Edition).* The Institute for Media Education. 2000.

Reisman, Dr. Judith A. "Images of Children, Crime and Violence in Playboy, Penthouse and Hustler magazines. A research booklet sponsored by the Office of Juvenile Justice and Delinquency Prevention, U.S. Department of Justice, Project No. 84-JN-AX-K007. November 1987.

Rimel, Rebecca. "Notes from the President: Useful Knowledge." *Trust* magazine. Spring 2006.

Scanlon, Terrence. "Buffet's Compassionate Calling." *Foundation Watch.* (Washington, D.C.) August 2006.

Schambra, William A. "Leftist Foundations Under Fire." *Chronicle of Philanthropy.* May 12, 2005.

Schlafly, Phyllis. "Scanning the News about North American Integration." *Phyllis Schlafly Report.* (Alton, Ill.) November 2006.

Schmitz, John G. "Abortionism. The Growing Cult of Baby Murder." *American Opinion*. (Belmont, Mass.) March 1974.

Schweizer, Peter. "Party of the Rich. Limousine Liberals Are Upgrading to Lear Jets." *National Review*. October 30, 2006.

Shawn, Eric. *The U.N. Exposed. How the United Nations Sabotages America's Security*. Penguin Group (New York) 2006.

SIECUS. "Position Statement on Sexually Explicit Materials." 1996.

Spann, James. "The Weather Channel Mess." Op-ed posted on *The Drudge Report* website. January 18, 2007.

Stelzer, Irwin. "The Gates-Buffet Merger. Billions Served" *The Weekly Standard*. July 17, 2006.

Stephens, Joe & Ottaway, David B. "IRS Toughens Scrutiny of Land Gifts." *The Washington Post*. July 1, 2004.

Stephens, Joe & Ottaway, David B. "Senators Question Conservancy's Practices." *The Washington Post*. June 8, 2005.

Stormer, John. *None Dare Call It Treason*. Liberty Bell Press. (Florissant, Missouri.) 1964.

"Strange Yokefellows:The National Council of Churches and its Growing Non-Church Constituency." Report by The Institute on Religion and Democracy. 2006.

"Strategic Philanthropy of Conservative Foundations. Moving a Public Policy Agenda." Report by the National Committee on Responsive Philanthropy. (2005).

Strode, Tom. "ECI Tries to Defend its Actions. Pro-Abortion Foundation Aided Evangelical Climate Effort." *Baptist Press*. May 1, 2006.

Strom, Stephanie. "ACLU Rejects Foundation Grants Over Terror Language." *The New York Times.* October 19, 2004.

Tooley, Mark. "Gore's God." *Crisis.* October 1996.

Usborne, David. "American Weather Forecasters Do Battle Over Mankind's Role in Global Warming." *The Independent.* January 19, 2007.

Walton, Jeff. "Evangelical Leaders Exploited by Global Warming-Population Control Lobby." WDC Media News. October 10, 2006.

Waugh, Joanna. "National Religious Partnership for the Environment." 1997.

Weaver, Warren. *U.S. Philanthropic Foundations: Their History, Structure, Management and Record.* (Harper and Row) 1967.

Weinman, Edward. "Going Nuclear. Interview With Patrick Moore." *Iceland Review.* November 13, 2006.

Wildovsky, Ben. "Generous to a Fault? A Close Look at Giving." *The Wall Street Journal.* January 11, 2007.

Wooster, Martin Morse. "The Ford Foundation's International Agenda." *Foundation Watch.* (Washington, D.C.) June 2004.

Wormser, Rene. *The Foundations: Their Power and Influence.* Covenant House Press. (Sevierville, Tenn.) 1993. (First published in 1958).

Yablonski, Christopher (editor). *Patterns of Corporate Philanthropy.* Capital Research Center. (Washington, D.C.) 2001.

# INDEX

169

# Also available by Phil Kent:

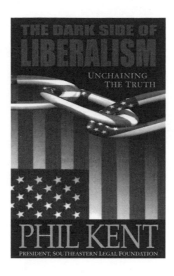

$24.95
9781891799099

*The Dark Side of Liberalism* offers a fresh look at America's big issues, devoting a chapter to each of our most controversial and frustrating concerns. Phil Kent describes the 'liberal line,' shares the good news about conservative success, and outlines effective techniques for fighting back in the courts, the media, and in our communities.

To order copies of this book or more copies of *Foundations of Betrayal*, contact your local bookstore or, if unavailable, contact us directly. Mr. Kent is also available for events and speaking engagements.

Contact:
Zoe Publications, LLC
P.O. Box 5294
Johnson City, TN 37602-5294
www.philkent.com